ROBERT BROWNING

ROBERT BROWNING

John Lucas

GREENWICH EXCHANGE
LONDON

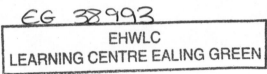
Greenwich Exchange, London

First published in Great Britain in 2003

Printed and bound by Q3 Digital/Litho, Loughborough
Tel: 01509 213456
Typesetting and layout by Albion Associates, London
Tel: 020 8852 4646
Cover design by December Publications, Belfast
Tel: 028 90352059

Cover: Detail of a portrait of Robert Browning by William Henry Grove
(1889) courtesy the National Portrait Gallery, London.

Greenwich Exchange Website: www.greenex.co.uk

ISBN 1-871551-59-5

For Peter Porter

Contents

Chronology

The dates of Browning's major publications are given throughout this study. Below are listed some of those not mentioned in the main body of the text.

1812   7th May, Browning born at Camberwell, London.

1828   Begins to attend newly formed University of London but soon leaves.

1833   *Pauline* privately printed. Makes no impact.

1835   *Paracelsus* published.

1837   *Strafford* published. Macready acts in its five-night run.

1838   First visit to Italy.

1840   *Sordello* published to howls of critical disapproval.

1841   *Bells and Pomegranates I: Pippa Passes* published.

1843   *A Blot in the 'Scutcheon* published and acted for three nights.

1844   Second visit to Italy.

1845   Meets Elizabeth Barrett.

1846   Marries Elizabeth Barrett and they leave England for Pisa.

1847   They settle at Casa Guidi, Florence.

1849   Son, Robert Wiedermann ('Pen') born.

1861   Death of Elizabeth Barrett Browning.

1861   Browning and his son settle at 19 Warwick Crescent, London.

1862   *Collected Poems* published (the so-called 'Third').

1881   Browning Society founded by F.J. Furnivall.

1888-9 'Fourth and complete edition' of *Collected Works*, carefully supervised by Browning.

1889   12th December, Browning dies in Venice. 31st December, buried in Westminster Abbey.

1 How he Struck his Contemporaries

Browning died in Venice on 12th December 1889. On the last day of the year he was granted his place in Poet's Corner at Westminster Abbey, and among those who crowded into the Abbey for the ceremony was Henry James. James had long been an intense admirer of Browning, whose massive novel-in-verse *The Ring and the Book* (1868) had exercised a profound effect on his fiction, but the English poet also puzzled the American novelist. In a short essay about the ceremony, James reflected that "A good many oddities and a good many great writers have been entombed in the Abbey; but none of the odd ones have been so great [as Browning] and none of the great ones so odd." What made Browning great was, James said, his "immense expression of life – of life rendered with large liberty and free experiment, with an unprejudiced intellectual eagerness to put himself in other people's place, to participate in complications and consequences; a restlessness of psychological research that might well alarm any pale company for their formal orthodoxies." Others have praised Browning in similar terms although few have put it as well. And the precise nature of these terms make plain why James the novelist should so admire Browning.

But what made Browning so very odd? Here, James is a bit coy, contenting himself with the suggestion that it has something to do with Browning having broken with "the tradition of the poetic character as something high, detached and simple." In his later years Browning had become decidedly attached to public and social life. Himself an inveterate diner-out, James knew very well that Browning was more familiar with and at dinner tables and salons than even he was. Browning had indeed become so much a social being that during his last years it was commonly remarked that he would die in his dinner jacket. The jacket has a part to play in James' story, 'The Private Life', where a famous writer of crushing obviousness dines out night after night while his doppelgänger pursues his art in private.

James' story was written in 1891, and this is significant not so much because it shows James worrying away at the puzzle of Browning as that his solution to the puzzle – the idea of the double – makes use of what by then had become a feature of contemporary thinking about the troubling nature of personality. (*The Strange Case of Dr Jekyll and Mr Hyde* had been published in 1886.) 'The Private Life' plays with the notion that two Robert Brownings inhabited the one skin: the hearty socialite and the great poet. And this make sense in terms of late 19th century assumptions about the artist as someone hugging the secret of his artistic temperament to himself, even if it would have puzzled Browning who, born in an earlier age, took the fact of being a writer rather more for granted than James was able to do.

Yet James' sense of Browning's oddness cannot be entirely disposed of by saying that if the poet doesn't conform to versions of the poet as typified by, for example, Swinburne or Yeats, this because their cultivation of artistic personality as indicating a man apart, singled-out from the mass, is developed long after Browning himself reached maturity. For it was not merely James who found Browning a puzzle. Here is Thomas Hardy, writing to Edmund Gosse in 1899. "The longer I live the more does B's character seem *the* literary puzzle of the 19th century. How could smug Christian optimism worthy of a dissenting grocer find a place inside a man who was so vast a seer & feeler when on neutral ground?"

That there is an occasional note of bluff cheerfulness in Browning's poetry can hardly be denied. Gerard Manley Hopkins had this in mind when he linked Browning with Charles Kingsley in order to imagine them as talking "with the air and spirit of a man bouncing up from table with his mouth full of bread and cheese and saying that he meant to stand no blasted nonsense."

Hopkins detested the kind of bullying common-sense he rightly found in Kingsley and which he attributed to Browning. Yet the very "air and spirit" he so deplored was in all likelihood what brought about the Browning Society. The Society was formed in 1881 with the express aim of first deciphering and then spreading the Master's message. As with other such societies that sprang up at around the same time, most notably perhaps the Society for Psychical Research, the Browning Society testifies to late 19th century attempts to rediscover the meaning of life in semi-religious terms, terms which Darwin's publications had seemingly erased. I suspect that Hopkins, whose remarks are contained in a letter to his friend W.R. Dixon dated 12th October 1881, is responding as a Catholic apologist to news of the Society's formation. Some years earlier, Matthew Arnold had suggested that poetry would be called upon to fulfil the function earlier undertaken by religion: to interpret the universe and to console mankind. The aim of the Browning Society was, according to its founder F.J. Furnivall, to prove that Browning "is the manliest, strongest, life-fullest, deepest, thoughtfullest of our living writers." It is not difficult to imagine Hopkins reading those claims and saying to himself, "bread and cheese".

Not that Browning is to be blamed for the Society, any more than he can be held to account for the fact that one of the earliest books about him, by Henry Jones, is called *Browning as a Philosophical and Religious Teacher* (1891). And we should note that members of the Society, keen though they were to extract messages from the poems, were sometimes compelled to admit that they simply couldn't understand them. Browning might be deep, thoughtful and strong, but he could also be difficult to the point of impenetrability. Nor were Society members alone in complaining of Browning's obscurity. In 1900 the American philosopher, George Santayana, published his *Interpretations of Poetry and Religion*, and in a chapter called 'The Poetry of Barbarism' he laid into what he saw as Browning's "failure in rationality and the indifference to perfection". Santayana was an admirer of Arnold, and he shared Arnold's belief, which had been set out in *Culture and Anarchy*, that the modern world stood in need of what Arnold characterised as the Hellenic spirit of sweetness and light and the pursuit of perfection. In a word, what the 19th century lacked was a belief in true Culture. There was far too much kow-towing to the "Hebraic" spirit. Energy, smoke, fire, muscularity. Admirable in their way, but lacking grace. Bread and cheese, in fact.

Santayana was convinced that the Hebraic spirit was at its worst in Browning's poetry. That poetry was remarkable for its "turgid style, weighty without nobility, pointed without naturalness or precision". In addition, when Browning tried to write about "personages" he produced only traits of character and never "... character as a whole". The philosopher was especially aggravated by Browning's inability, as he saw it, to write well about Italy. The poet could not imagine the "civilised heart" of the Italian Renaissance. "He saw, he studied, and he painted a decapitated Italy. His vision could not mount so high as her head." Santayana, it will be apparent, had an idealising cast of mind. Browning didn't. Nor for that matter did Ruskin. And Ruskin considered that more than any other English

3

writer, Browning captured the Renaissance spirit – "its worldliness, inconsistency, pride, hypocrisy, ignorance of itself, love of art, of luxury, and of good Latin." Ruskin has especially in mind lines from 'The Bishop orders His Tomb', and discussion of that poem must wait its turn. But here it is worth noting that much more recently Peter Porter has remarked that "Browning ... was able to imagine the Italy of the great days of the New Learning, which were also the less great days of the decline of the Communes into signorial despotism, as no English poet, except Shakespeare, had done."

Well, Renaissance Italy is a place of the imagination, Santayana's no less than Ruskin's or Porter's, or of course Browning's. Santayana thought Browning was unaware of the "civilised heart" in 15th century Florence, because he possessed no civilised mind and therefore no matching style. Small wonder, therefore, that his poetry should be "turgid ... weighty without nobility." It was certainly like nobody else's. It was also so distinctive that it readily lent itself to parody. Hence, for example, C.S. Calverley's 'The Cock and the Bull':

> Then fumbled at, and stumbled out of, door,
> I shoved the timber ope wi' my omoplat;
> And *in vestibulo*, i'the lobby to-wit,
> (Iacobi Faccioloati's rendering, sir,)
> Donn'd gallaskins, antigropeloes,
> And so forth ...

Browning's insatiable love affair with unusual words, which Calverley mocks in "gallaskins" and "antigropeloes", could get him into trouble, most famously when he has his innocent heroine, Pippa, sing of "owls and bats, cowls and twats". (Browning assumed that the word, which he'd found in an obscure 17th century text, was an item of nun's clothing.) More seriously, his flinty, harsh-sounding language could become, as G.K. Chesterton acknowledges, "grotesque", like the excrescences of Gothic architecture. But Chesterton, whose study of Browning, published as long ago as 1903, seems to me still one of the best books ever written about Browning, brilliantly exonerates this grotesqueness from the charge of accidental ugliness. Though he is prepared to admit that Browning could and did write badly, he also insists that the grotesque is properly intrinsic to

4

Browning's best poetry. As Chesterton says, "the essential issue about Browning as an artist is not whether he, in common with Byron, Wordsworth, Shelley, Tennyson, and Swinburne, sometimes wrote bad poetry, but whether in any other style than Browning's you could have achieved the precise effect which is achieved by such incomparable lyrics as 'The Patriot' or 'The Laboratory'. The answer must be in the negative, and in that lies the whole justification of Browning as an artist."

There are, it should be said, other justifications for Browning's poetry which, to be fair to him, Chesterton goes on to acknowledge. Chief among them perhaps are Browning's insatiable curiosity about human behaviour and his love of formal experimentation, or what Chesterton calls his "fierce hunt after poetic originality." This occasionally leads him into very strange territory indeed. Some poems have a kind of distorted, manic ingenuity, as though Edward Munch is being re-invented by Max Brod. Such poems are truly and unsaveably grotesque. This is the price Browning is ready to pay for taking risks that other, less ambitious and better "balanced" poets would be keen to avoid. But as he has Andrea Del Sarto remark, "a man's reach should exceed his grasp,/ Or what's a Heaven for?" Most great poets, when they write badly, write dully. But Browning is never dull and one reason for this is that he is always trying to extend his grasp. To put it rather differently – to put it in Bishop Blougram's words – "My business is not to remake myself." Browning is always trying out new subjects. Not only that. I can think of no poet apart from Thomas Hardy who comes near him in the search after formal novelty, and not even Hardy can equal the wondrous rhymes of 'The Pied Piper of Hamelin' or the Gothic verve of 'Childe Roland to the Dark Tower Came'. Here, as elsewhere, Browning is quite simply unique.

2   The Early Years

Robert Browning was born on 1st May 1812, in Camberwell, South London. Some three months earlier, on 7th February to be exact, Charles Dickens had first seen the light of day. The proximity of birth dates is worth remarking, not merely because Dickens and Browning would become the two greatest English writers of the 19th century, but because they had much else in common. "Meredith is a prose Browning and so is Browning." Oscar Wilde's would-be witticism is intended to link the work of writers whom their contemporaries typically found to be both difficult – all that knotty, tortuous syntax – and prosaic. There are points of comparison, but none so remarkable as those that exist between Browning and Dickens. It would have made far better sense for Wilde to have remarked that Browning is a poetic Dickens and so is Dickens. Dickens is certainly the great poet of the English novel, his language more richly metaphoric than any writer bar Shakespeare. He is also a writer of the utmost energy and one of omnivorous curiosity. Even a fragment of Browning's poetry, Chesterton said, leaves "the impression of a certain eternal human energy. Energy and joy." He might have been speaking of Dickens.

But the two are connected by more than artistic temperament. Neither was the product of a university education. Dickens left school at the age of 16. At the same age Browning began to attend classes at London University, but he did not complete a session. Both were however formidably well-read, and not merely in the literature and ideas of their own country. Browning was the more accomplished linguist (French, Italian, German, Greek, Latin, Hebrew), but Dickens (French, Italian, some German, some Latin) knew more about the New World. In addition, both were drawn to the theatre. Dickens, who briefly considered the possibility of becoming a professional actor, was a most accomplished amateur, and his famous reading tours were by all accounts triumphs of histrionics. (They also hastened his death.) Like Browning, he wrote for the theatre. In 1836 he had two plays on in London, *The Strange Gentleman*, and *The Village Coquettes*. In that year he first met John Forster, who was to become a life-long friend and his biographer, although in 1836, Forster, who had written in praise of *The Pickwick Papers*, was more concerned to find a publisher for Browning's *Sordello* and in persuading William Macready, perhaps the most famous actor of his day, to stage the poet's *Strafford*. He succeeded in his latter effort, and the following year the play was produced at Covent Garden, with Macready in the title role.

Macready may well have been won over because, as an ardent republican, he welcomed the chance to act the part of Charles I's betrayed minister in a play about the corruptions of monarchy. For 1837 was the year of Victoria's coronation, an event many believed and hoped would never occur. The anticipated death of William IV would, it was widely assumed, bring the British monarchy to a natural close. Instead, 'Miss Guelph' became queen. Browning had been a republican at least since 1826, when he first read Shelley. (As a result he was also converted to vegetarianism and atheism.) He may have been led to Shelley by his early friendship with W.J. Fox, a friendship which had begun two years earlier, and which was to be hugely important to him in his formative years. Fox, who had been born in 1786 and who died in 1864, was an ardent admirer of Shelley. He had started life as a weaver's boy, become a fiery Unitarian preacher, was a radical republican, a feminist (he and his wife lived apart and from 1834 Fox cohabited with his ward, Eliza Flower, herself a keen admirer of Mary Wollstonecroft), a socialist, journalist and, crucially, editor of *The Monthly Repository*, which before it ceased publication in 1838, brought together many of the best radical writers of the day, some of whom would migrate to Dickens' *Household Words* at the end of the following decade. Among them was R.H. Horne.

Like them all, Horne was a passionate admirer of Shelley. His verse drama *Orion* was dubbed "the farthing epic" when it appeared in 1843 because Horne sold it for that amount in order to encourage the poorest of readers to buy the poem. In 1834 he published a 'burlesque' presumably intended for the stage although it seems never to have been produced. *The Spirit of Peers and People* is, according to Horne's biographer Ann Blainey, "a vicious attack on church, king and parliament." Quite so. The ending goes so far as to prophesy imminent violent revolution. "Gold is God and labour is the Ass/ But now 'tis riddent to the precipice." The choice is either for peaceful change or "the flow of fratricidal blood,/ Ruin, or injury."

Horne needs to be mentioned in any discussion of Browning, because the two, who first met in 1835, share a Shelley-inspired radicalism which defined the Fox circle. And this is the sustaining subsoil for everything Browning writes. The heroine of his first publication, the anonymous *Pauline* (1833), in which Shelley is extolled as "the great sun-treader", is, so the editor of the reliable Penguin two-volume *Poems* tells us, modelled probably on "Eliza Flower, or possibly her sister Sarah, or a fusion of the two – the friendship of the Flower sisters ... meant much to [Browning]". Ten years after meeting Horne, and probably through his agency, Browning met Elizabeth Barrett, who lived in the same street as the 'Farthing Poet', and who had been in correspondence with him since 1839. She had by then published 'The Cry of the Children', a poem based on her appalled reading of Horne's report into the condition of the child labourers in South Staffs. The poem brought her some fame. In addition, Fox championed her cause. One of the many lectures he gave in London during 1843-4, and which were gathered together in two volumes as *Lectures Intended Chiefly For the Working-Classes*, was devoted to Poets of the Day, and Fox made a point of singling out a number of women poets for special mention, including Elizabeth Barrett.

When Browning met Barrett she was therefore better known than he was. Not that he was an entire unknown, but his reputation was by no means secure. He had produced *Paracelsus*, a poem of 5 Parts and over 4000 lines, in a six-month burst in 1835, the publication of which earned him what his Penguin editors call "A modicum of fame". As with *Pauline,* the influence of Shelley – especially *Alastor* – is unmistakable. *Paracelsus* takes as its subject the inspirations of a great soul and in this it anticipates a number of late-Romantic epics which infest the 1840s and 50s, and are known collectively as "Spasmodic" poems. Browning's poem, however much it sprawls, is a great deal more readable than Philip James Bailey's *Festus* (first published 1839, revised and expanded in later editions, of which there were too many), or Sydney Dobell's *Balder* (1853), both of them indebted to Browning. But although he remained proud of *Paracelsus* and revised it carefully in 1849 and again in 1868 and 1888, there is something gaseous about it, not merely in the sense that it seems over-inflated but because the subject is ungraspably vague. Browning seems to have feared that this might be so, because he added a Preface in which he says that:

> I am anxious that the reader should not ... judge [the poem] by principles on which it was never moulded, and subject it to a standard to which it was never meant to conform. I therefore anticipate his discovery, that it is an attempt, probably more novel than happy, to reverse the method usually adopted by writers whose aim it is to set forth any phenomenon of the mind or the passions, by the operation of persons and events; and that, instead of having recourse to an external machinery of incidents to create and evolve the crisis I desire to produce, I have ventured to display somewhat minutely the mood itself in its rise and progress, and have suffered the agency by which it is influenced and determined, to be generally discernible in its effects alone, and subordinate throughout, if not altogether excluded ...

Which at the very least shows that Browning could be as difficult in prose as in verse. More interestingly, these words show him anticipating the Jamesian credo that character determines action rather than the other way round. The emphasis is on 'mood', on what might be called the psychological weather of the aspiring Paracelsus. Outer events count for far less.

But if this makes for difficulties in *Paracelsus* they are as nothing compared to the problems caused by *Sordello*. This massive poem was published in 1840. Browning apparently began work on it before turning to *Paracelsus*, and its lengthy gestation may help to explain its deformities, chief among which is undoubtedly obscurity. Ezra Pound claimed to understand it, although he never explained his explanation. The poem's first readers, few in number, were unanimous in admitting defeat. I once thought I knew what the poem was about and in *Literature and Politics in the Nineteenth Century* (1971) said as much. According to the young Lucas, *Sordello* "takes up the problem of how the poet is to be a communicator and whether communication can ever be socially meaningful." Not only that: Browning on the one hand wants to criticise Sordello for keeping apart from issues of the day, but on the other he accepts the "possibility that only by contemplative withdrawal can the poet become true to himself and his vision." I suspect that I took the will for the deed, although it seems fair enough to imagine that, both as a member of Fox's circle of radicals and a Shelleyan, Browning would find himself having to think through the question of art's relationship to society. What now strikes me about *Sordello* is less its possible meaning than the care with which Browning establishes the poem's Italian context. Dante had had Sordello as his guide in the *Purgatory* (vi-ix). Browning would have known this, of course, and for further information would, so John Pettigrew says, have consulted the *Biographie Universelle* and a host of studies of the Italian Renaissance.

And this is where matters become a good deal more interesting. Browning first visited Italy in 1838. He was already fascinated by the place, which, given his adoration of Shelley, should come as no surprise. But Browning's Italy was very different from Shelley's. Shelley, the ardent idealist, saw in Italy a symbol of hope for the future of mankind. Italy was where the West Wind blew its message of renewal, it was where the freed Prometheus, aided by Demogorgon, that underground spirit of violent energy, threw off the shackles of servitude and emerged into a world of affiliative love. But Browning saw Italy in quite different terms. He was of course sympathetic to the still-deferred dream of liberation from Austrian control and of making a new nation. But his study of the Renaissance had inevitably opened his eyes to the contradictions of a period Santayana would later regard as the dream of civilisation made flesh. Like Shelley, Santayana was an idealist, although unlike Shelley he was deeply conservative. In sharp distinction from either, Browning saw the Renaissance as at time of glitter and squalor, of noble ideals and princely psychopaths, of high morals and low living.

Pippa Passes is perhaps Browning's first attempt to engage these contradictions. This 'closet-drama', as it has been called, was written in 1841, and seems to have been intended for the stage, possibly as an opera. We know that Browning, who was massively knowledgeable about music and deeply committed to the art, hoped to write an opera, and we also know that he suggested to Eliza Flower that she compose music for the play's lyrics. As far as I am aware she did not take up his suggestion, and although the play has been performed on a few occasions, it cannot be thought of as any more a success than Browning's other attempts at dramatic writing. These include *The Return of the Druses*, which he had pressed Macready to produce, even apparently pursuing the unfortunate actor-manager to his bath in his effort to get the play staged, and *A Blot in the 'Scutcheon*, published in 1843. This play includes the line "I had no mother to protect me, so I fell", which at one time was almost as famous as Mrs Henry Wood's "Dead and never called me mother", from *East Lynne*, which it may indeed have inspired.

Pippa Passes owes much to Browning's 1838 visit to Italy, when he fell in love with "delicious Asolo" as he called it, an ancient hill town, some thirty miles north-west of Venice. "All the play's locations are from direct observation", Pettigrew remarks. He also quotes Browning's friend, Mrs Orr, as saying that the idea for the drama occurred when Browning was walking alone in a wood near Dulwich, and "the image flashed upon him of some one walking thus alone through life; one apparently too obscure to leave a trace of his or her passage, yet exercising a lasting though unconscious influence at every step of it; and the image shaped itself of the little silk-winder of Asolo, Felippa, or Pippa." This very strikingly anticipates an element deep at the heart of Dickens' great novel *Little Dorrit*. But there similarities end. *Pippa Passes* would have greatly benefited from the addition of music. Without it, the supposedly redemptive impact of the "little silk-winder's" songs on assorted human types seems hopelessly sentimental.

Browning was not quite thirty when he published *Pippa Passes*. Judging by quantity alone, he had by then produced a substantial amount of work, although nothing he had written could really be said to mark him out from others – apart that is, from the super-abundant energy necessary to carry through such huge enterprises as *Paracelsus* and *Sordello*, the latter of which weighed in at very nearly 6,000 lines. Yet in an age when aspiring poets were lured into epic pretensions, such energy, while remarkable, was by no means unique.

But then, in 1842, Browning published a collection of individual poems called *Dramatic Lyrics*, and in its pages, all at once, a great poet burst into view. The poems that make up the collection had been written over a number of years. Browning's publisher now sensibly urged him to bring them together, and even more sensibly recommended that he didn't lump them in with some of his plays. *Dramatic Lyrics* amounts to no more than a pamphlet of 16 poems, the third in a series brought out under the general title of *Bells and*

Pomegranates, all paid for by the poet's father. There was no great disgrace in this. By the time Browning began publishing, poetry had for the most part ceased to be commercially successful. It's hey-day coincided with the time of the Napoleonic Wars, when Walter Scott made a near fortune from publishing narrative poems before turning to novel writing, and when Byron's *Childe Harold* became a huge best-seller and John Murray paid even George Crabbe 3,000 guineas for his *Tales of the Hall* (1819).

By 1842 it was novelists rather than poets who were making large sums of money from their writing. Still, at least two collections published in that year became vastly popular and continued to be reprinted throughout the century. One was Macaulay's *Lays of Ancient Rome;* the other, Tennyson's two-volume *Poems*. This included a number of revised versions of poems from his 1833 collection – among them, 'The Lady of Shallott" and 'The Lotus Eaters' – plus 'Ulysses', 'Break, Break, Break' and 'Morte d'Arthur'. *Poems* not only established Tennyson's reputation, it made him indisputably the most popular as well as the most successful poet of the latter half of the 19th century.

Dramatic Lyrics in comparison attracted little notice and sold poorly. Nevertheless, it is every bit as important in declaring a great, original poet, as was Tennyson's two-volume collection. For in its pages are to be found 'Waring', 'Soliloquy of the Spanish Cloister', 'The Pied Piper of Hamelin', 'Porphria's Lover', 'Artemis Prologizes' and, above all, 'My Last Duchess'. It also contains 'Incident of the French Camp' and 'Cavalier Tunes'. The three poems that make up the Tunes were probably written in the year of the pamphlet's publication, the tercentenary of the outbreak of the English Civil War. The opening Tune 'Marching Along' ends:

> Then, God for King Charles! Pym and his snarls
> To the Devil that pricks on such pestilent carles!
> Hold by the right, you double your might;
> So, onward to Nottingham, fresh for the fight.
>
> CHORUS – *March we along, fifty-score strong,*
> *Great-hearted gentlemen, singing this song!*

1842 was a year in which royalists and their sympathisers worked especially hard to popularise the monarchy. It was also the year of the second great Chartist uprising. The first such uprising, which had taken place three years earlier, was widely seen at the time as the possible harbinger of revolution. It hadn't succeeded then, but that wasn't to say it might not succeed in the near future. Hence the need to have people feel that God was on the side of Victoria. But as events at Nottingham would have reminded Browning's readers, this wasn't how the Deity chose to show himself in 1642. The royalists were trounced.

But if Browning's republicanism can be sensed in these tongue-in-cheek songs for King Charles, his radicalism doesn't stop there. It is important that 'My Last Duchess' follows immediately on the Cavalier Tunes. Browning for the first time here sets poem against poem in order to ironise or question the import of each. This becomes integral to *Men and Women* (1855), but it matters in *Dramatic Lyrics*, too. We can hardly avoid sensing how the man who speaks 'My Last Duchess' has an aristocratic hauteur that goes with his insistence on male supremacy. The Commonwealth period had been one in which radical sects had taken sexual equality for granted, and I have noted that the Fox circle was wholly committed to the Rights of Women.

Not so the Duke of Ferrara:

> That's my last Duchess painted on the wall,
> Looking as if she were alive. I call
> That piece a wonder, now: Fra Pandolf's hands
> Worked busily a day, and there she stands.

Browning had used narrative couplets throughout *Sordello* in order to give a forward momentum to his tale. The refusal to use end-stopped rhyme in that poem had frequently led to what seemed whole paragraphs speeding by before you could draw breath. Here, the Duke's suave manner is at one with the use of rhyme as a means to direct attention to the implications of all he says. In a headnote to his pamphlet, Browning remarks: "Such Poems as the majority in this volume might also come properly enough, I suppose, under the head of "Dramatic pieces"; being, though often Lyric in expression, always dramatic in principle, and so many utterances of so many imaginative persons, not mine." This requires some comment.

'I suppose' – In his diffident reference to 'Dramatic pieces' Browning is drawing attention to a poetic genre which is now more customarily known as the dramatic monologue. Whether he invented this kind of poem continues to be subject for debate, one that has been ably addressed by Robert Langbaum in *The Poetry of Experience* (1957) and more recently by Isobel Armstrong in *Victorian Poetry: Poetry, Poetics and Politics* (1993). As both of these commentators recognise, Tennyson has at least as good a claim as Browning to be the onlie begetter of a genre which after all includes his 'Ulysses'. On the other hand, Browning seems to me the genre's greatest exponent and in 'My Last Duchess' he produces a poem that is as original as it has proved influential for later poets, from T.S. Eliot onwards.

'My Last Duchess' is a dramatic monologue that reveals all the Duke intends his hapless auditor and, then, us to know about him – chiefly that under the sophisticated courtesies he is not a man to be disobeyed nor displeased. It also betrays his sadistic pleasure in making people bend to his will as well as a paranoid fear of being opposed. (Especially by women.) And we are made to register these matters entirely through what the Duke has to say. It is *here*, rather than in his plays, that Browning shows himself a great master of dramatic speech. He also shows himself a master of historical imagination. George Santayana would not allow this to be so. Where is the "civilised" element of the Italian Renaissance in Browning's poetry, Santayana asked rhetorically. The answer is that it is amply testified to in the taste and elaborate formality of the Duke of Ferrara as he saunters along his gallery, pointing out especial treasures to his guest who, it eventually turns out, has come to negotiate on behalf of the bride-to-be's father. Try crossing me and you're done for, he means. You can hear the menace in his voice, its lethal promise, as you come round the line ending at "and I choose/ Never to stoop." The stress on the word "Never" tells all we need to know about this man's ruthlessness.

Such unyielding ferocity of intent is fuelled by sexual jealousy, the at-a-remove voyeurism which causes him to imagine the Duchess looking favourably on Fra Pandolf, that "faint/ Half-flush that dies along her throat." How does he *know*? The answer of course is that he doesn't. In poem after poem Browning reveals himself as a poet of sensuous detail. He is also a master of the specifically erotic and of the heart and mind's crooked ways in love. Here, the Duke, encased in his steely will, can never allow himself to surrender to what Auden would call "the varied action of the blood". How can he, when he takes his viciousness to be virtue: it is bound up with, is an expression of, his aristocratic poise. Nothing must be allowed to ruffle this poise, as the emissary to whom he speaks is required to infer. And so, having made the matter as clear as he needs, the Duke says:

> I repeat,
> The Count your master's known munificence
> Is ample warrant that no just pretence
> Of mine for dowry will be disallowed;
> Though his fair daughter's self, as I avowed
> At starting, is my object. Nay, we'll go
> Together down, sir. Notice Neptune, though,
> Taming a sea-horse, thought a rarity,
> Which Claus of Innsbruck cast in bronze for me!

"I repeat". Not in our presence, he hasn't, which, as with the remark about what he avowed at starting, makes plain that we have come in on the middle of a conversation – or, more accurately, monologue. And he is as studiously civil at the end as when we first hear him, telling the Count's emissary that his master's reputation for generosity means that he, the Duke, can expect to receive all the dowry he'll ask for; and then adding – it's not quite an after-thought – that naturally he's more interested in the Count's daughter, as "object". At which point you can imagine the emissary may be hoping to slip away and tell his master not to sacrifice his daughter to this monster. For why otherwise should the Duke say "Nay, we'll go/ Together down, sir", as though he's placed a restraining hand on the poor man's shoulder? And having secured him, he once more makes him consider an art object and, therefore, the impeccable taste of its owner-connoisseur. This is where we came in.

In his brilliant essay, 'Browning's Important Parleying', Peter Porter remarks that "Browning's immediate influence was negligible. Despite the Browning Societies and the flurry he made in literary circles, he had no immediate followers, other than Eugene Lee-Hamilton. His effect was like a time bomb. His great influence began to manifest itself only in the Nineteen Twenties." This is undoubtedly true if you think of his influence on poets. But if you think of novelists the question of Browning's influence is rather different. We know for example that George Eliot was a deep admirer. In January, 1856, she wrote at length in the *Westminster Review* about the recently published *Men and Women*, remarking that Browning's "keen glance pierces into all the secrets of human character, but ... he reveals those secrets, not by a process of dissection, but by dramatic painting." And she comments that "'Fra Lippo Lippi' is better than an essay on Realism in Art; we would rather have 'The Statue and the Bust' than a three-volumed novel with the same moral." I cannot prove that when George Eliot came to write about Grandcourt, the husband of Gwendolen Harcourt in *Daniel Deronda* (1876), she had Browning's Duke in mind; but Grandcourt, a monster of "marital absolutism" in the words of Graham Handley, the novel's most recent editor, is also a sadist who exhibits "a dislike of confrontation, a tendency to exert his power almost at one remove from his presence or at least without the compulsion of noise and action." Moreover he is "used to having his reflexive absolutism obeyed without question." This could well be a description of the Duke of Ferrara.

It could also be a description of Gilbert Osmond, the egotistic monster who marries Isobel Archer. Henry James' *Portrait of a Lady* (1881) undoubtedly revisits George Eliot's novel in its study of a marriage in which a free spirit is ground "in the very mill of the conventional"; but where Grandcourt is an Englishman at home in England, James, whose devotion to Browning is beyond question, makes Osmond an aesthete living in self-imposed exile in Italy where he collects people as he collects *objects d'art*. Once married to him, Isobel is to become the very Portrait of a Lady. When we first meet her after her marriage, she is seen by a hapless admirer, Rosier, himself a collector of trifles, "coming out of the deep doorway. She was dressed in black velvet; she looked high and splendid ... his appreciation of her ... was based partly on his eye for decorative character, his instinct for authenticity; but also on a sense for uncatalogued values, for that secret of a 'lustre' beyond any recorded losing ..." (ch 37). Though Rosier regards Isobel as a work of art, he is also sensitive to "uncatalogued values". Osmond, on the other hand, puts her on show as proof of his supreme good taste. His ruthless egotism, his contempt for Isobel as a flesh-and-blood woman, his desire always to maintain the poise he thinks goes with aesthetic preference – all this echoes much that is first explored in Browning's great poem.

There are even faint after-echoes of such egotism in Forster's *A Room with A View* (1907) where Cecil Vyse is, like Grandcourt and Osmond, both an aesthete and a snob who despises anyone without his sense of aesthetic regard, and who wants his fiancée, Lucy Honeychurch, to conform to his idea of the beautiful. When she suddenly loses her temper with him, Cecil thinks that "she had failed to be Leonardesque ... her face was inartistic."

All these novels have contemporary settings and owe a debt to what in the later years of the 19th century became commonly called "the marriage question". In steep contrast 'My Last Duchess' is set in 16th century Ferrara. Yet it is also a contemporary poem in the sense that it addresses the issue of masculinity, an issue closely associated with the "manliness" promoted by the new public schools. Raymond Williams has characterised this as a matter "of what Manly was coming to mean ... What was taught and learned was a new and rigid control, 'self-control'." Put that beside something J.S. Mill says in *The Subjection of Woman*, which he wrote at the beginning of the 1860s, about how women "are brought up from the earliest years in the belief that their ideal of character [lies in] submission and yielding to the control of others" and it is clear that Browning's poem acts as a crucial intervention in a gathering ethos, a hardening orthodoxy of approved relationships between the sexes. (Dickens shows himself deeply attentive to and critical of this orthodoxy in his study of his major protagonist's relations with his wives and daughter in *Dombey and Son* (Written 1846-48.))

'Italy' as 'My Last Duchess' was originally called, was at first coupled with a poem then known as 'France' and later as 'Count Gismond'. This poem is spoken by a wronged wife saved from her husband, Gauthier, (who has accused her of adultery), by the Count. Gismond gives Gauthier the lie, they fight, and after Gauthier is killed the pair escape south. At the very end of the poem, which is made up of 21 six-line tetrameter stanzas rhyming ababcc, we understand that the narrator has been telling her story to another woman. She is interrupted by her husband's sudden appearance:

> Gismond here?
> And have you brought my tercel back?
> I was just telling Adela
> How many birds it struck since May.

I quote these lines, not because they are especially good or belong to a poem of outstanding merit, but to draw attention to Browning's great ability at shaping a conversational note within the requirements of formal metre. This is one of the great glories of English literature, but, Byron and Crabbe apart, it had been lost to sight since Pope. Browning's skill in making use of speech rhythms is another reason why he so appealed to the great 19th century novelists, especially as for him speech is not merely an indication of social register but reveals or betrays the speaker's psychology or indeed psychopathology.

'Count Gismond' has a further significance in that its initial link to 'My Last Duchess' means that a woman's voice follows a man's, and that two very different versions of love are therefore set against each other. And although Browning broke the link here as he did for all those poems in *Dramatic Lyrics* which he'd at first coupled (they include 'Incident of the French Camp' and 'Soliloquy of the Spanish Cloister', and 'Rudel to the Lady of Tripoli' and 'Christina'), we should note that in future collections he will deliberately position poems back-to-back in order to disturb any fixed view or conviction. Those editors who have chosen to disregard his ordering of poems have therefore acted with gross irresponsibility. They have denied the poems' true meaning.

This bears especially on Browning's greatest collection, *Men and Women*, but it also affects *Dramatic Lyrics*, even though the coupling of poems here is for the most part opportunistic. This is certainly the case with 'Incident of the French Camp' and 'Soliloquy of the Spanish Cloister' – France and Spain – because the former is simply a tale of heroism in action while the latter is a minor *tour-de-force*, an hilarious, over-the-top account of one man's seething hatred for another, as though Gavin Ewart and Sean O'Brien had joined forces to produce a competition-winner on the subject of office politics:

> At the meal we sit together:
> *Salve tibi*! I must hear
> Wise talk of the kind of weather,
> Sort of season, sort of year:

Not a plenteous cork-crop: scarcely
    Dare we hope oak-galls, I doubt:
What's the Latin name for 'parsley'?
    What's the Greek name for Swine's Snout?

At this moment in the 19th century, England abounded in good light poets, chief among them perhaps Thomas Hood and W.M. Praed. 'Soliloquy of the Spanish Cloister' may not be light verse but it makes plain how wonderfully accomplished Browning was at handling the kind of stanza which in other hands would be reserved for the merely comic.

It is followed by 'In a Gondola'. This poem, like Maclise's painting 'The Seranade' that prompted it, rejoices in the northern cliché of Venice as the city of love, often, as here, of illicit love. A man and a married woman revel in their sexual attraction to each other and at the end of the poem "He is surprised, and stabbed." There is something decidedly operatic about both the setting and the treatment of the subject, and the sensuality (which Browning will return to in one of his greatest poems 'A Toccata of Galuppi's') begs to be accompanied by music. We are told at one point that "She Sings" the following:

I
The moth's kiss, first!
Kiss me as if you made believe
You were not sure, this eve,
How my face, your flower, had pursed
Its petals up; so, here and there
You brush it, till I grow aware
Who wants me, and wide ope I burst.

II
The bee's kiss, now!
Kiss me as if you entered gay
My heart at some noonday,
A bud that dares not disallow
The claim, so all is rendered up,
And passively its shattered cup
    Over your head to sleep I bow.

There used to be a tedious commonplace, which is still trotted out by lazy-minded commentators, that as the 19th century wore on, so writers ceased to be able to write about sex. No. The truth is that they found increasingly subtle ways of treating the subject. This song is a good example.

In the poem that follows, 'Artemis Prologizes', a woman also speaks, although unlike the unnamed woman of 'Love in a Gondola', Artemis is the embodiment of chastity:

> I am a goddess of the ambrosial courts,
> And save by Her, Queen of Pride, surpassed
> By none whose temples whiten this the world.

Browning apparently contemplated writing a sequel to Euripedes' *Hippolytus*, about Medea's incestuous passion for her stepson. Given his other attempts at drama we should probably be grateful that the project was abandoned. But there is excellent reason to applaud this prologue, whose blank verse is handled with massive assurance. It is yet another instance of Browning declaring his technical prowess, and even if we think 'Artemis Prologizes' no more than an exercise, we must add that it is a 'masterpiece' in the Renaissance sense of that term: the poem has been sent out from the Browning workshop to advertise what he can do. This includes the ability to do Milton almost as well as Milton. Hence:

> Hippolutos exclaiming in his rage
> Against the fury of the Queen, she judged
> Life insupportable; and, pricked at heart
> An Amazonian stranger's race should dare
> To scorn her, perished by the murderous cord:
> Yet, ere she perished, blasted in a scroll
> The fame of him her swerving made not swerve.

The polysyllabic words, the powerful verbs, the positioning of key words at line-endings (judged, dare): this is all grandly Miltonic. No wonder Matthew Arnold, for whom Milton was all grand style, should have so admired the poem.

'Artemis Prologizes' is dressed-up as "poetry". It is sonorous, stately, a bit phoney. And this is emphasised by the following poem, 'Waring', which in a quite astonishing change of tone begins:

What's become of Waring
Since he gave us all the slip,
Chose land-travel or seafaring,
Boots and chest or staff or scrip,
Rather than pace up and down
Any longer London town?

Throughout this 260 line poem Browning moves with nonchalant aplomb between three and four stresses. 'Waring' is a casual, tongue-in-cheek tale of a someone apparently destined for great things in the world of art who, in words Philip Larkin used of a not dissimilar subject, "chucked up everything/ And just cleared off." But whereas Larkin's 'Poetry of Departures' is serious about its subject, 'Waring' is serious about its treatment. It is one more proof of how Browning the technician can manage to write well in just about any verse form.

Technical brio and daring were undoubtedly features of much 19th century poetry and they have not always met with approval. When Donald Davie delivered an on-the-whole reserved judgement on Thomas Hardy, he said that Hardy's love of a wide variety of verse forms could be accounted for as *superbia*, which he likened to Victorian civil engineering. The forms weren't in other words organically necessary, but arbitrarily chosen to show off technical expertise. There was no *intrinsic* reason, Davie implies, why so many 19th century public buildings – prisons, schools, hospitals, factories – should look as they did. And by the same token there was no *intrinsic* reason for the shape of many of Hardy's poems. This ignores or anyway underrates playfulness as an element in art, let alone that delight in doing difficult things well that is often and betrayingly confused with lack of seriousness, dilettantism. More importantly, both Hardy and Browning, from whom Hardy learnt so much, work in different styles and forms because only by such means can they find how to handle a wide variety of subject matter. One style can only do so much. For some poets – Milton, Pope and Wallace Stevens spring to mind – this is more or less enough. For others, such as Auden and Browning, it isn't. Auden developed different styles over a long career. The truly extraordinary thing about Browning, as *Dramatic Lyrics* shows, was that at any time he could work with equal ease in various styles, forms, voices.

And so from 'Waring' we move to 'Rudel to the Lady of Tripoli', written in narrative pentameter couplets, and from there to the poem with which it was at first coupled, 'Christina', each of its eight stanzas made up of eight trochaic tetrameter lines, in which the ingenious feminine rhymes are taken by the even lines. The two poems are linked by Browning's handling of the kind of love to which Goethe had given the term "elective affinity." As developed in Goethe's novel *Lotte In Weimar*, "elective affinity" amounts to far more than love at first sight. The "affinity" Goethe has in mind is an almost Platonic concept of two people perfectly complementing, indeed completing, each other. Made for each other, as the cliché has it. Yeats, who for long believed in such affinity between himself and Maud Gonne, spoke of how their two youthful natures "blent ... Into the yolk and white of the one shell" (in 'Among School Children'). But probably the most famous expression of this affinity in the whole of English literature is the cry, "Nelly, I *am* Heathcliff."

Wuthering Heights was published in 1847 as was *Jane Eyre*, in which the relationship between the heroine and Rochester can also be thought of in Goethian terms. This is emphatically not to argue for Browning's influence over either novelist; it is merely to suggest a community of interest, one that becomes evident when the male speaker of 'Christina' claims that the look that passed between him and the woman was enough to put beyond doubt that at that moment "Mine and her souls rushed together." But, he immediately goes on:

> Oh, observe! Of course, next moment,
>   The world's honours, in derision
> Trampled out the light for ever ...

As with the Bronte sisters' novels – and we might add the relationship between Pip and Estella in *Great Expectations* – social division threatens and may overwhelm the affinity of souls the speaker here testifies to. And such apparent affinity may become murderous, as it does in 'Porphria's Lover', where the man strangles the loved woman in order to keep her forever faithful. Here, the speaker unwittingly reveals himself as a man whose determination never to share his lover may be diseased but is by no means unusual, then, now, ever. On most days you can read a newspaper report of some trial where a man stands accused of murdering his wife, mistress, partner, "out of love", because he feared she was about to leave him. "And if I can't have her, nobody will." The speaker of Browning's poem doesn't quite say that. He does, however, remark that Porphria murmured:

> how she loved me – she
> Too weak, for all her heart's endeavour,
> To set its struggling passion free
> From pride, and vainer ties dissever,
> And give herself to me forever.

But he then reflects that she has after all come through wind and rain to be with him, so that "at last I knew/ Porphryia worshipped me." Worshipped? Theirs is not then a relationship which implies equality of love; "worshipped" throws an ironic after-light on those "vainer ties" he hasn't persuaded her to dissever herself from. This is monstrous vanity and it is therefore significant that 'Porphyria's Lover' comes immediately after 'Johannes Agricola in Meditation', for this poem is spoken by a man who thinks himself one of God's elect. The Penguin editor remarks that "Browning had no sympathy… with doctrines of predestination, eternal damnation, salvation by faith alone, election and so on." Browning was also aware that, just as in 19th century England there was no lack of men who thought as Porphryia's lover did, and who indeed were prepared to act as he had, so Johannes Agricola's equivalents were unctuously claiming to "bargain for [God's] love, and stand/ Paying a price, at his right hand."

After these two poems comes the slight 'Through the Metidja to Abd-el-Kadr', which was apparently extemporised while Browning was out horse riding. It would be possible to compile a thick anthology of English horse riding poems, including of course Browning's own 'How They Brought the Good News from Ghent to Aix', but all that needs to be said of this particular example is that it testifies to Browning's radical interest in the struggles for national independence which were then continuing to spread across the known world. Shelley had ardently supported the cause of Greek and Italian liberation from oppressive foreign powers; Abd-el-kadr, Emir of Mascara, fought for Algerian independence from France, and in the summer of 1842 suffered some heavy defeats. Browning's speaker is imagined as riding to the Emir's aid.

And with that inconsiderable poem *Dramatic Lyrics* was meant to end. As the pamphlet was going to press, however, Browning was told that there were still some blank pages to fill. Might he perhaps have an extra poem to plug the gap? As it happened, he had, although he was far from certain that the poem he handed over was appropriate. It was after all a poem meant for children.

'The Pied Piper of Hamelin' had been written in May 1842 to entertain William Macready's oldest son, then ill in bed. Browning suggested the boy should illustrate the poem, and in many subsequent editions 'The Pied Piper' has indeed been accompanied by illustrations, although so far as I am aware Macready's have not survived. Under the title Browning wrote "A Child's Story" and added a dedication ("Written for, and inscribed to, W.M. the Younger.") Presumably he was hoping to ward off adult readers who might have been offended by the poem's inclusion. In the event, and as the endless illustrated re-prints show, 'The Pied Piper of Hamelin' gradually established itself as a children's classic.

The 19th century was the great age of children's literature. As the book industry developed so this potentially rich market was bound to be targeted. And as Romantic belief in the integrity of the child's imagination increasingly took hold, so literature for children changed from the homiletic hymns and cautionary tales common in the 18th century to the more purely fanciful, untrammelled work of the middle and later years of the 19th century. Not that 'literature with a message' entirely disappeared. It survives even in the better work, including – to take examples more or less at random – Charles Kingsley's *Water Babies* (1863) and R.M. Ballentyne's mid-century adventure stories for boys which, rollicking yarns of sea-faring though they may be, are also about the imperial spirit as a combination of Roman fortitude and English gallantry, with a dash of chivalry thrown in for good measure.

'The Pied Piper of Hamelin' has its moral. It is however purely tongue-in-cheek. At the very end, Browning addresses the boy to whom he's dedicated the poem:

> So Willy, let you and me be wipers
> Of scores out with all men – especially pipers.
> And whether they pipe us free from rates or from mice,
> If we've promised them aught, let us keep our promise!

Even Chesterton winced at this utterly outrageous, almost unsayable rhyme. But that is the point. It's a final joke. You can imagine Browning, who throughout has rhymed with such inventive exuberance as to take anyone's breath away, (no-one, not even Kit Wright, can do it better) speaking these lines to the young boy and inviting him to wonder what on earth the closing rhyme can be. And when he delivers "promise", with the stress on the second syllable whose vowel has to be twisted to bring it into line with "mice", it's like a grotesque pun or an absurdly far-fetched, ridiculous play on words. Exactly what children love, in fact.

They certainly came to love the poem. And no wonder. It is a great story, and the shifting of rhythms, of line-length, the paying out of linked chains of rhyme, not only testify to Browning's technical dazzle, as though you're in the presence of the most consummate verbal prestidigitator, they are done with such glee that the poem becomes a joyous feast of language – including handsful of out-of-the-way words – and metre, on which he plays just about every variation. Browning also supplies a haunting sense of the land of Cockaigne to which the children are led, where "The sparrows were brighter than peacocks here,/ And their dogs outran our fallow deer,/ And honey-bees had lost their stings,/ And horses were born with eagles' wings". He even touches on a subject of age-old fascination, the lost or wandering tribe, who may be the descendents of the children led away by the piper. In this case the tribe is located in Transylvania. It would be, wouldn't it?

3 Dramatic Romances and Lyrics

Three years after *Dramatic Lyrics*, Browning published the seventh
in the *Bells and Pomegranates* series that, like the rest, was paid for
by his father. The book runs to very nearly a hundred pages in the
two volume Penguin edition and is made up of poems which for the
most part had been composed in the years 1842-45. Among the best
known are 'How They Brought the Good News from Ghent to Aix',
of which Browning had later to confess that he hadn't the faintest
idea what the good news was – he also had difficulty remembering
the opening lines when, in the year of his death, he came to recite the
poem into an Edison cylinder; and 'The Lost Leader'. Of this, he
remarked that while he didn't mean to accuse Wordsworth of changing
politics because of money considerations, the great poet's "regular
about-face of his special party, was to my juvenile apprehension,
and even mature consideration, an event to deplore."

Almost as famous and far better than these two much anthologised
poems are 'Home-Thoughts, from Abroad', 'Meeting at Night' and
'Parting at Morning', and 'The Bishop Orders His Tomb at Saint
Praxed's Church'. Ruskin's praise of this, well known though it is,
and part of which I quoted in my opening chapter, deserves to be set
out here in full. "I know no other piece of modern English, prose or
poetry," Ruskin wrote in *Modern Painters, IV,* "in which there is so
much told, as in these lines, of the Renaissance spirit, – its worldliness,
inconsistency, pride, hypocrisy, ignorance of itself, love of art, of
luxury, and of good Latin. It is all that I said of the central Renaissance
in 30 pages of *Stones of Venice*, put into as many lines, Browning's
being also the antecedent word."

Like the lesser 'Pictor Ignotus' in the same collection, 'The Bishop
Orders His Tomb' is a monologue. The speaker of 'Pictor Ignotus' is
a 16th century Florentine journeyman artist, resigned to a life of
painting "These endless cloisters and eternal aisles/ With the same
series, Virgin, Babe and Saint,/ With the same cold calm beautiful
regard." His only consolation is that "At least no merchant traffics
in my heart." He means that he wants no truck with those who buy
and sell art without thought for its intrinsic worth, who "prate" of
how "'This I love, or this I hate,/ This likes me more, and this affects

me less!'" Browning is here touching on an important matter. For it was during the 1840s that the marketing of contemporary art in England took on new urgency. The rise of what Carlyle called the plutocracy, of newly enriched industrialists, manufacturers, bankers, merchants, was accompanied by various shows of wealth and of freshly attained respectability. And what could be more respectable, more a vindication of the taste of men of the nouveaux riches, than the pictures they hung on their walls or, for that matter, the statues they stood in their salons? Parlour statuary was all the rage. Prince Albert was known to have acquired some examples. (The newly-established *Art Journal* carried up-to-date information on who was buying what.) The buying of contemporary art was equally the rage of the time. And of course there were experts to tell the rich what to buy. Dickens was quickly on to this.[1] Hence, Mr Dombey's sudden interest in "appurtenances" – furniture, carpets, paintings, statuary – intended to show him in the best possible light as connoisseur, although all he owns has been chosen for him by his manager, Carker, since Dombey himself couldn't tell a Greuze from a Grimshaw.

Dombey and Son was being written at about the time that Browning published 'Pictor Ignotus'. I mention this, not to imply any influence of one great writer over the other, but to suggest that both are alert to currents running strongly in those years and that Browning's view of Renaissance Italy is inevitably affected by them. This, it will be remembered, was what displeased Santayana. But you could turn his criticism on its head and say that precisely because Browning was so attentive to certain features of mid-19th century life, he was alerted to similar features of the social and cultural life of Renaissance Italy, where connoisseurship was similarly prevalent. Browning's cast of mind may have made him uneasy with idealising, but it didn't lead him to cynicism. He is too aware of the corrugations of the heart for that, has greater tolerance for foibles, a more generous, speculative interest in what people are than any cynic can achieve. 'Pictor Ignotus' – it means painter unknown – ends with the artist's voice speaking out of history:

> So die my pictures! surely, gently die!
> O youth, men praise so, – holds their praise its worth?
> Blown harshly, keeps the trump its golden cry?
> Tastes sweet the water with such specks of earth?

Like any creative person, the unknown artist who speaks here reveals that he started out with high hopes of achieving immortality through his art, even dares to say at the beginning of his monologue that "I could have painted pictures like that youth's/ Ye praise so" – the youth in question being almost certainly Raphael. Now, he faces the sad certainty of being erased from the future's regard.

Not so the Bishop who orders his tomb:

> Vanity, saith the preacher, vanity!
> Draw round my bed: is Anselm keeping back?
> Nephews – sons of mine ... ah God, I know not! Well –
> She, men would have to be your mother once,
> Old Gandalf envied me, so fair she was!
> What's done is done, and she is dead beside,
> Dead long ago, and I am Bishop since,
> And as she died so must we die ourselves,
> And thence ye may perceive the world's a dream.

As these opening lines reveal, The Bishop is a magnificent old rogue. Even when he's wondering whether to deny that he's the father of his "nephews" he can't help boasting about the beauty of their mother. "Vanity" has a meaning here that outsoars his routine piety. He may say the world's a dream but never was it fleshier, more one of appetency. Even as he mouths the words of Ecclesiastes, "Man goeth to the grave, and where is he", he's thinking of how his tomb will make Gandalf "see and burst" with envy:

> Did I say basalt for my slab, sons? Black –
> 'Twas ever antique-black I meant! How else
> Shall ye contrast my frieze to come beneath?
> The bas-relief in bronze ye promised me,
> Those Pans and Nymphs ye wot of, and perchance
> Some tripod, thyrsus, with a vase or so,
> The Saviour at his sermon on the mount,
> Saint Praxed in a glory, and one Pan
> Ready to twitch the Nymph's last garment off,
> And Moses with the tables ...

No matter how many times I've read these lines, the man's sheer effrontery, his insatiable relish for the material world, always make me laugh out loud. And at the poem's very end he asks to be left in peace:

> That I may watch at leisure if he leers –
> Old Gandolf at me, from his onion-stone,
> As still he envied me, so fair she was!

Hypocrite is too mean a word for the Bishop. Like Falstaff he over-flows moral categories.

Mid-19th century art in England, the art produced by men at least, was pestered by a kind of frustrated sensuality. As a result, Browning's sensuousness, his eroticism, feels to be a world apart from what his male contemporaries were painting, carving or writing. Some years ago Jerome McGann suggested that Monckton Milnes' 1840s edition of Keats tended in its textual preferences to emphasise Keats' Georgian (male) taste for voyeuristic fantasising in a manner that bordered on the pornographic. (Milnes was a well-known collector of erotic and pornographic works.) McGann developed this line of thinking at a time when 'the male gaze' was itself coming under intense scrutiny. The Bishop makes no bones about his enjoyment of such gazing. Hence for example, his request to have carved on his tomb "mistresses with great smooth marbly limbs". It could of course be argued that, such were the conventions of the times, not much more than gazing was permitted to men in mid 19th century England. But in fact England didn't become 'Victorian' until rather later. It's rather that among the middle and upper classes, a concept of manliness was gaining ground, aided by the new public schools, as a result of which the sensuous was somehow seen as beneath male dignity. Interestingly, there is no English equivalent for *L'homme moyen sensuel*, although I imagine the phrase is of English origin, and its Frenchness 'proof' that we wouldn't tolerate such things here. Browning is not at all what is meant by the phrase, but he is an intensely erotic poet. This gives him an assuredness when he writes of men like the Duke of Ferrara for whom male sexuality is power, an exercise in authority and, therefore, suppression; it also makes his own love poetry unlike that of any other 19th century English poet, although Shelley at one end and Hardy at the other come close.

There will be more to say about Browning's intense love for Shelley. Here, I want only to suggest that the poet he once called "the great Sun-treader" would have at once recognised the fineness of 'Meeting at Night' and 'Parting at Morning'. The first is vivid, immediate, alive with the urgency of anticipation:

I
The grey sea and the long black land;
And the yellow half-moon large and low;
And the startled little waves that leap
In fiery ringlets from their sleep
As I gain the cove with pushing prow,
And quench its speed i' the slushy sand.

II
Then a mile of warm sea-scented beach;
Three fields to cross till a farm appears;
A tap at the pane, the quick sharp scratch
And blue spurt of a lighted match,
And a voice less loud, through its joys and fears,
Than the two hearts beating each to each.

Each stanza is made up of a single sentence uttered in the continuous present, each drives towards a conclusion which is charged with sexual energy, and the second goes so far as to imply a consummation devoutly to be wished.

But: love by night, work by day. 'Parting at Morning' is a mere four lines long:

Round the cape of a sudden came the sea,
And the sun looked over the mountain's rim:
And straight was a path of gold for him,
And the need of a world of men for me.

In 1889 Browning explained to a questioner that the last line meant "it is *his* confession of how fleeting is the belief (implied in the first part) that such raptures are self-sufficient and enduring – as for the time they appear." The urgency with which the man had steered to his love is matched by the urgency of his "need" to rejoin the world of men. In both cases he goes 'straight' to his target, although in 'Meeting at Night' we sense an almost painful joy in the man's registering of physical details, so alert are his senses, whereas in the four lines that make up the second poem the urgency is connected to a summons to things of this world. The tide will not wait for him, will carry him away on the "path of gold". I may be over-reading here but there is surely a hint that the world of men is a world of business, of golden guineas. The woman, in contrast, belongs to an almost secret world, hidden from the eye. She is no longer at the forefront of his needs.

To say this may seem to indicate that for the man love is, to quote Byron's famous words, "a thing apart." And you could undoubtedly see the relationship as a clandestine one, the meeting by night necessarily secretive. But my own view is that, while we cannot identify Browning and the speaker of the poem as one and the same person, the two poems at least allow the poet to touch on a matter that similarly infuses the love poetry of Shelley and Hardy, namely, the way in which moonlight, or candle- or lamplight, is connected with a visionary awareness of the loved one, which daylight – the light of common day – dispels. I don't want to reduce this to the schema of gender difference/opposition: moon = Artemis or Diana, female principle: sun = Apollo or Phoebus, male principle. Browning's poems are in no sense reductive. But the fact of difference is part of their meaning.

In a much more playful mode he explores difference in 'Nationality in Drinks' where, for example, Tokay jumps up "on our table":

> Dwarfish to see, but stout and able,
> Arms and accoutrements all in order;
> And fierce he looked North, then, wheeling South,
> Blew with his bugle a challenge to Drouth ...

These lines, with their comic personification, are reminiscent of the exuberant ingenuity of certain illustrative artists of the 19th century, especially George Cruikshank, whose Comic Alphabet, for example, plays wondrous games with the possibilities released by letters. I'm also reminded of the habit of vivid personification to be found in Christopher Smart, (1722-1771) a poet whom Browning read and admired, although hardly anyone else at the time knew about "mad Kit Smart". (But then Browning's omnivorous reading took him to poets entirely unknown to most of his contemporaries.) Smart's "Strong Labour got up with his pipe in his mouth/ And stoutly strode over the vale" would be calculated to appeal to the poet who can image Tokay as "Twist[ing] his thumb in his red moustache/ ... Shrugg[ing[his hump-shoulder, to tell the beholder/ For twenty such knaves he should laugh but the bolder."

'Nationality in Drinks' is a comic tour-de-force. And 'Home-Thoughts, from Abroad' is an equally dazzling technical accomplishment, in rhyme, metrical variation, and syntactical structure:

> Hark, where my blossomed pear-tree in the hedge
> Leans to the field and scatters on the clover
> Blossoms and dewdrops – at the bent spray's edge –
> That's the wise thrush;

Hark. And you listen while over three lines the poet tracks the sound to source and then, round the line-ending, comes his voice, exultant: "*That's* the wise thrush." There is no need to make great claims for these two poems, but I wouldn't be without either of them.

'Christmas-Eve' and 'Easter-Day', on the other hand, published in 1850, is not a work to which I feel any need to return. I will believe the critics and biographers who say that the two companion poems were written after the death of Browning's pious mother in March 1849 and the birth of his son in the same month; and I can accept that, as Pettigrew and Collins tell us in the Notes to their Penguin Edition, the poet "is working out his own religious beliefs in the poems, after a long period in which those beliefs had been far from settled; and Browning speaks here more directly (as his wife had urged him to do) than is customary." But I am not surprised that the work, while inevitably of interest to the specialist and biographer, sold poorly.

Footnotes
[1] Page 27 – Dombey's taste in art, which tamely follows 'informed' taste of the 1840s, is an important matter and one that need to be considered in any adequate account of 'Pictor Ignotus'. For more on this see the detailed Appendix B, 'The Illustrations to Dombey and Son', in the 1980 edition of my *The Melancholy Man: A Study of Dickens' Novels*, Harvester Press.

4   *Men and Women*

Browning's next collection had no more commercial success. *Men and Women*, to give this great collection its proper title, was published in 1855, by which time a good deal had happened to Browning to change him from the poet who a decade earlier had published *Dramatic Romances and Lyrics*. He was now married, a father, and living with his wife and son in Italy. What hadn't changed was their relative fame. Of the two poets, Elizabeth Barrett Browning was by far the better known and more highly regarded. An enlarged edition of her two-volume *Poems*, which had first appeared in 1844, was published in 1850 to considerable acclaim, and her love poems to her husband, 'Sonnets from the Portuguese', came in for especial praise. In both Italy and in France the Brownings had witnessed the stirrings and then suppression of democratic revolutionary movements, although they reacted differently to events in the two countries. Both identified with the cause of Italian independence and grieved as its advances were rolled back in 1849. But Browning was on his own in supporting the cause of French Republicanism. His wife did not join him in cursing Louis Buonaparte when the emperor-to-be's soldiers massacred French citizens in the winter of 1851.

The Brownings witnessed this violence at first hand because at the time they happened to be staying in Paris, where Robert was finishing his essay on Shelley. In this, he distinguishes between two kinds of poet: the objective, stirred by outer events, and the subjective, guided by the inner light of his own imagination. Browning saw in Shelley a supreme example of the latter – and for him – superior type. Yet he knew that Shelley, the author of 'Ode to the West Wind', 'The Mask of Anarchy' and 'Prometheus Unbound', to name three obvious examples, was the ardent champion of Liberty and Republican ideals. While she was expressly on the side of those fighting for Italian independence, his wife appears to have had little sympathy with French Republicans. (Franco-phobia was a way of life for most English intellectuals during the 19th century.) She described them as "a little popular scum, cleared off at once by the troops". Robert, on the other hand, was deeply stirred by the brutality of Louis Buonaparte's troops. But although he saw what was happening he neither did nor said anything.

So at least his biographers seem to agree. They are wrong. The opening poem *of Men and Women* is called 'Love Among the Ruins'. The setting is a place of unkempt pastures, "the site once of a city great and gay". Here, two lovers meet. Browning's concern is mostly with the place and its history. The last stanza runs:

> In one year they sent a million fighters forth
> > South and North,
> And they built their gods a brazen pillar high
> > As the sky,
> Yet reserved a thousand chariots in full force –
> > Gold, of course.
> Oh heart! oh blood that freezes, blood that burns!
> > Earth's returns
> For whole centuries of folly, noise and sin!
> > Shut them in,
> With their triumphs and their glories and the rest!
> > Love is best.

It would be difficult to imagine a plainer statement of detestation for military glory, or a more naked avowal of the superior claims of Love, the Beloved Republic.

Here, then, it is crucial to note that *Men and Women* appeared during the Crimean War, that prime example of "folly, noise and sin", as George Russell's dispatches from the front line to *The Times* of London were making clear. (The charge of the Light Brigade, folly's *primus inter pares*, occurred on 25th October 1854). It never ceases to amaze me that of the dozens of critical studies of Browning I've read, not one mentions the significance of his placing 'Love Among the Ruins' at the front of *Men and Women*. It doesn't matter whether he had the events of December 1851 specifically in mind when he wrote the poem, the date of whose composition is unknown. Betty Miller says it was conceived in January 1852, the night after 'Childe Roland to the Dark Tower Came', which would suggest a direct link to events of the previous month, but other commentators are more cautious, and there is no need to tie it to any one event in order to understand why Browning chose to place the poem at the head of a collection published in 1855.

There is reason to suppose that critics and readers of the time sensed the significance of this, even if they did not directly confront it. For *Men and Women* was for the most part indifferently received. The review in the *Athenaeum*, which appeared on publication day, 17th November 1855, is typical. "Who will not grieve over energy wasted and power misspent", the reviewer asks rhetorically, and then goes on " – over fancies chaste and noble, so overhung by the 'seven veils' of obscurity, that we can oftentimes be only sure that fancies exist." It is the same old story, one repeated by virtually all who bothered to review the collection. Browning was unwarrantably difficult, he lacked mellifluousness, he was uncouth, barbaric, unnatural. The two-volume edition sold badly, copies were still available years later, and there was no second edition. In the words of Pettigrew and Collins, "Browning continued to be known as his wife's husband."

The near uniformity of this response ought to make us wince at our own critical certainties. For *Men and Women* is one of the glories of English literature, containing a number of poems that are among the greatest of its or any century. Merely to list them is to feel a kind of awed wonder at the impercipience, malice, misprision, the lord knows what, of Browning's reviewers. 'Fra Lippo Lippi', 'A Toccata of Galuppi's', 'By the Fire-Side', 'Childe Roland to the Dark Tower Came', 'Respectability', 'A Light Woman', 'The Statue and the Bust', 'How it Strikes a Contemporary', 'The Last Ride Together', 'Bishop Blougram's Apology', 'Andrea del Sarto' … on and on the list goes. Looking at these titles, running over in my mind the many others that could be added, I think of Randall Jarrell contemplating the misjudgements of former days and saying ironically to fellow critics, "*Brothers, we'd* never make the same mistake, would we". No, we'd make different ones.

Nevertheless, the failure of Browning's contemporaries to understand how much he'd achieved in *Men and Women* is difficult to explain. A few years earlier, Arthur Hugh Clough, another much underrated poet (now as then), remarked that novelists were doing rather better than poets in coming to terms with their age. With *Bleak House* especially in mind, Clough noted that "our novelists give us a real house to live in". The same can be said of Browning. The characters and settings of his poems have a physicality, a palpable presence, that is the quintessence of realist art, and without straining for comparisons it is not at all unreasonable to link his name with such great contemporaries as Gustave Courbet (1819-1917) and Jean Francois Millet (1814-1875). It may even be that Browning's English critics were alarmed by the unabashed sensuousness of his writing, and especially his candid eroticism, both of which elements were important in the work of the two French painters.

This eroticism isn't especially evident in 'Love Among the Ruins', which is more intent on delineating militarism's creation of a desert of uniformity, to use a phrase of E.M. Forster's, who probably had in mind the "lone and level sands" of Shelley's 'Ozyzmandias'. Behind all these lies the Roman historian Tacitus' great, sad lament: "they make a desolation and they call it peace". Hence, we might infer, the apparently unopposable statement with which Browning's poem concludes. "Love is best." War destroys, but Love flourishes like the green bay tree. Yet, as always with Browning, matters then turn out to be not so simple. The next poem in the collection is called 'A Lovers' Quarrel' The apparently unqualified assertions of one poem are challenged, confronted, even denied by the next. This is a tactic employed on other occasions in *Men and Women*. Poems that oppose each other's affirmations are deliberately placed back to back in order to set up a dialogue, even a dialectic. It is therefore infuriating to discover that over the years editors have repeatedly monkeyed about with the order of the poems and as a result have part-destroyed their meaning. To take one example. When Browning followed 'Respectability' by 'A Light Woman' he knew exactly what he was doing. The first poem is about the disreputability of two lovers, at all events when their relationship is seen from a conventional point of view. The second, in which a respectable man speaks, lays bare what is truly disreputable in his conventional attitude to a woman's sexuality. The speaker of 'Respectability' is a man speaking to a woman, his lover. As with 'Meeting at Night', we can, if we want, imagine the lovers to be engaged in a clandestine affair. They are in Paris, away from the proprieties of "the world", which term I take to be Browning's way of defining the moral conventions of mid-century England, or as much of those as London society comprehends. (When Pope spoke of "The World" in *The Rape of the Lock*, he similarly shrank the universe to London's bon ton.):

I

Dear, had the world in its caprice,
> Deigned to proclaim 'I know you both,
> Have recognized your plighted troth,
Am sponsor for you: live in peace!' –
How many precious months and years
> Of youth had passed, that speed so fast,
> Before we found it out at last,
The world, and what it fears?

From which we can infer that their relationship is a fully sexual one, although the tone of this opening stanza is one which blends quizzical amusement with great tenderness. They'd try to make us respectable by keeping us 'pure', the man is saying, but imagine:

> How much of priceless life were spent …
> Ere we dared wander, nights like this,
> > Through wind and rain, and watch the Seine,
> > And feel the Boulevart break again
> To warmth and light and bliss?

The word 'wander' hints here at a transgressive act that takes the lovers from the conventional straight and narrow. Wandering is what you do when you aren't ready to accept the rules and confinements of respectable behaviour. In other words, the term (and title) 'Respectablity' is being used ironically in the poem, which itself would be seen as a dangerous move by some of Browning's contemporaries. They would have been especially shocked by the poem's third and last stanza; but then course he *wants* them to be shocked:

> I know! The world proscribes not love;
> > Allows my finger to caress
> > Your lips' contour and downiness,
> Provided it supply a glove.
> The world's good word! – the Institute!
> > Guizot receives Montalembert!
> > Eh? Down the court three lampions flare:
> Put forward your best foot.

This is both daring and entirely proper. Supply a "glove" and keep love chaste, not of the flesh. The extreme sensuousness of the second and third lines surely indicates that the couple are lovers in the full sense of the word, in need of no covering. (Although in echoing Donne's word – and Browning read Donne, as he read Smart, at a time when nobody else was doing so – I need to add that there is no trace in 'Respectability' of the aggressive triumphalism that marks Donne's 'On His Mistress, Going to Bed'.) The poem's last lines are the nearest we come, not to triumphalism but to a kind of benign indifference for the world's notion of what constitutes Respectability. Browning is here referring to the ceremony held at the French Academy on 5th February 1852, at which, Pettigrew and Collins tell us, the poet "was apparently present, [when] Francois Guizot had to welcome his enemy Charles Montalembert" into membership. If that's respectability, the speaker says, then our love is infinitely preferable. There is a world elsewhere. At any time 'Respectability' is a fine poem, but I like to think that its impact would have been especially powerful in 1855.

'A Light Woman' which follows, is spoken by a very different man, one who is the very model of rectitude, male dignity, and – we come to understand – fear and loathing of any woman who shows herself as sexually alive. Near the poem's end we are made to understand that he is speaking to Browning himself, "you writer of plays", and his (melo)dramatic tale concerns a young male friend of his whom he's decided to save from a woman of experience, a predator on the look-out to corrupt innocence. This, anyway, is how the man sees her: she "crossed his path with her hunting-noose/ And over him threw her net." To prove to his friend the fact and extent of her wiles, the speaker therefore pretends to fall for her himself: "How easy to prove to him, I said,/ An eagle's the game her pride prefers,/ Though she snaps at a wren instead." The image transforms her from huntress to giant bird of prey. It also betrays the speaker's consummate vanity. He's a true eagle. And in case his listener has missed the inference, he adds: "The eagle am I, with my fame in the world,/ The wren is he, with his maiden face." So now we know. The young man would have stood no chance, but with the seasoned warrior:

> she lies in my hand as tame
> As a pear late basking over a wall;
> Just a touch to try and off it came;

> 'Tis mine, — can I let it fall?

> With no mind to eat it, that's the worst!
>> Were it thrown in the road, would the case assist?
> 'Twas quenching a dozen blue-flies' thirst,
>> When I gave its stalk a twist.

(stanzas ix-x)

This is the key moment, for it is here the speaker most fully betrays himself. Woman as pear: the image has an ancient lineage, partly because, visual reasons aside, to the male imagination ripeness is, if not all, then much to be desired. And so, when Jude Fawley talks to his friend Gillingham about Sue Bridehead's return to Philotson, Gillingham says, "Well, you've all but got her again at last ... The pear has dropped into your hand." (*Jude the Obscure*, part six, ch. v.) Hardy knew his Browning, but the phrase had general currency. In 'A Light Woman' its use is such as to make plain the speaker's pathological fear of the woman, as the truly shocking line "'Twas quenching a dozen blue-flies' thirst" reveals. Moreover, the speaker's attempt to explain and exonerate himself is, it become equally plain, based on suppositions. In other words, it comes from his deeply conventional reading of his friend as virginal – needing to be saved from a wicked woman, whose wickedness is meant to be taken on trust. (*He* says she's a seductress, so she must be!)

Henry James' story, 'The Lesson of the Master', uses the essence of Browning's great poem in order to develop a teasing account of the possible need for an artist to save himself (or to be saved) for his art. In this story, a writer of mature years seduces a woman away from a younger, aspiring writer. We never know whether he does this because he genuinely wants to save the younger man, or because he fancies the woman for himself, or for that matter sees her as a possible source for regenerating his own life as writer. Nor can we be sure that either man's devotion to art is compromised by his involvement with a woman. We can, however, be certain that Browning, a feminist in theory and in practice a devoted husband, is in effect cauterising a great sore of mid-19th century British manhood. At the very end of the poem, the speaker admits as much:

> Well, any how, here the story stays,
>   So far at least as I understand;
> And, Robert Browning, you writer of plays,
>   Here's a subject made to your hand.

He's as good as admitting that his and therefore other men's confident 'knowledge' of women is misplaced. That editors were either blind to or upset by the meaning Browning wished the two poems to convey is evident from the fact that they have so often been separated from each other. It is as though the poems had to be tamed.

II

It is easy to understand why Hardy so greatly admired the poem that follows 'A Light Woman'. 'The Statue and the Bust' is in effect a Satire of Circumstance. The setting is Renaissance Florence, Dante's city, and Browning perhaps honours the great Italian poet in using *terza rima* for his own poem, although his four-stress lines, with their adroit mix of iamb and anapest, are handled with a lightness of touch that's very different from the music of *The Divine Comedy*. The poem seems to be harking back to the idea of love as elective affinity that had engaged Browning in poems discussed in the previous chapter:

> He looked at her, as a lover can;
> She looked at him, as one who awakes:
> The past was a sleep, and her life began.

Who are they? She, a princess promised in marriage to another man, he, the Great-Duke Ferdinand, friend to the bride-to-be's husband. We seem to be set up for a tale of romantic derring-do, of lovers fleeing and finding love (or death) in each other's arms. But no. The marriage goes ahead, the Duke and the Lady continue at a distance from each other, enjoying the *schadenfreude* of their lost love and, as a way of commemorating it, deciding that their youthful images should be perpetuated, he by means of a statue, she through the carving of a bust. At the end of this tale of what didn't happen, the narrator imagines how their spirits ponder "What a gift life was, ages ago." But they have turned their backs on the gift:

I hear you reproach, 'But delay was best,
For their end was a crime.' – Oh, a crime will do
As well, I reply, to serve for a test,

As a virtue, golden through and through ...

Do your best, whether winning or losing it ...

If you choose to play! – is my principle.
Let a man contest to the uttermost
For his life's set prize, be it what it will!

The counter our lovers staked was lost
As surely as if it was lawful coin:
And the sin I impute to each frustrate ghost

Is – the unlit lamp and the ungirt loin,
Through the end in sight was a vice, I say.

Dante locates the adulterous lovers, Paolo and Francesca, in the second circle of hell. He knows they must suffer, but it feels as though he doesn't want them to suffer the worst torments hell can provide. Browning's speaker does not specifically recall these two, but he offers a most unchristian suggestion that the "frustrate" lovers he has talked of would have been better to have lived all they could. These are not his words, though, they come from the mouth of Strether, the lonely protagonist of Henry James' *The Ambassadors*, who adds "it's a great mistake not to."

Although we need not identify poet and narrator in Browning's poem, Strether's words, or something like them, seem to hover about 'The Statue and the Bust'. Yet a doubt remains. *Was* it a mistake to choose a life of conventional virtue over one of romantic excess? That we find ourselves confronted by this question should not surprise us. For casuistry – "the application of general ethical principles to particular moral problems, especially where conflicting obligations arise" – provides the spark for many of Browning's finest poems. It both warms and illuminates 'Bishop Blougram's Apology' and his great novel in verse, *The Ring and the Book*. Nevertheless, there does seem to be a deep distrust of prudential values running through *Men and Women*. From this comes, for example, 'The Last Ride

Together', in which the male speaker voices a genial contempt for those who prefer a life of public duty and honour, or of devotion to an abstract cause, to his choice of living for the moment:

> We ride and I see her bosom heave.
> There's many a crown for who can reach.
> Ten lines, a statesman's life in each!
> The flag stuck on a heap of bones,
> A soldier's doing! What atones?
> They scratch his name on the Abbey-stones.
> My riding is better, by their leave.

Whether Yeats had Browning's poem somewhere within his imagination's earshot when he came to write 'Easter 1916' I don't know, but in that great poem he powerfully contrasts those who live to seize the day with those who devote their lives to a cause, and chooses for his image of instinctual life:

> The rider, the birds that range
> From cloud to tumbling cloud,
> Minute by minute they change;
> A shadow of cloud on the stream
> Changes minute by minute;
> A horse-hoof slides on the brim,
> And a horse plashes within it …
> Minute by minute they live:
> The stone's in the midst of all.

Browning's rider isn't brutishly tied to a life of sensual pleasure (although some commentators have seen his joy in 'riding' as explicitly sexual); he even allows himself to ask "Who knows what's fit for us?" But the question isn't entirely rhetorical, for his answer comes down on the side of "Earth being so good." As Robert Frost said, "Earth's the right place for love:/ I don't know where it's likely to go better." But is it? This is the question that threads its way through 'A Toccata of Galuppi's'.

This poem comes immediately after 'Fra Lippo Lippi', one of the greatest of those monologues of which Browning was an accomplished master, and on which I must comment before I try to do justice to the 'Toccata'. Fra Lippo Lippi is both monk and artist, and, like the Bishop of St Praxed's, a lover of pretty women. In Fra Lippo Lippi's case, though, we can surely find no trace of hypocrisy in his candid enjoyment of flesh. He says to the man he's addressing:

> Your business is not to catch men with show,
> With homage to the perishable clay,
> But lift them over it, ignore it all,
> Make them forget there's such a thing as flesh.
>
> (11s 179-182)

This is a far cry from his business, however:

> Or say there's beauty with no soul at all –
> (I never saw it – put the case the same –)
> If you get simple beauty and naught else,
> You get about the best thing God invents:
> That's somewhat: and you'll find the soul you have missed,
> Within yourself, when you return him thanks.
>
> (11s 215-220)

Moreover, as he later confesses:

> I always see the garden and God there
> A-making man's wife: and, my lesson learned,
> The value and significance of flesh,
> I can't unlearn ten minutes afterwards.
>
> (11s 266-269)

Browning is here alluding to an issue that greatly troubled the Church during the 15th century (Lippi was born c1406 and died in 1469): the extent to which art should concern itself with realistic depiction of the flesh, especially naked flesh. Mightn't such art lead to idolatry of the merely human and away from contemplation of the Divine? Browning, who took many details in this monologue from Vasari's *Lives of the Artists*, is undoubtedly sympathetic to Lippi's position, one that has more in common with Blake's praise for the human form divine than it does with the early Renaissance Church. In the words of E.D.H. Johnson, "Fra Lippo Lippi ... paints by instinct; and what he paints is the world of his perceptions, not an intellectualised abstraction of it ... underlying the intensity of his response to human experience is the innate perception of a higher reality made manifest,

43

if at all, through the appearances of this world." In the poem that follows it is the contrast between earthly and heavenly, or perhaps the knowledge – or fear – that there is no heaven which brings an especial sadness, even agony of discontent, to the speaker. This leads us to 'A Toccata of Galuppi's'.

The imagined setting of this great poem is not Renaissance Florence but 18th century Venice. Moreover, the man who does the imagining is a 19th century Englishman. There will be more to say about this. Before that, however, I need to say a little about the poem's metre. 'A Toccata of Galuppi's' is written in trochaic octameter, that is in eight-stress lines, each foot of which reverses the usual iambic pattern of English verse in which an unstressed is followed by a stressed syllable. ("To be or not to be".)

There is a foolish and ignorant claim, first made by Ezra Pound and still parroted by his more uncritical followers, that poetry of the period 1830-1900 was in thrall to the iambic pentameter. Nothing could be further from the truth. The great 19th century poets were endlessly experimental in formal matters and I do not think that we can separate such experiments from their desire to break out of the confines of orthodoxy, or at least to test its limits: social, sexual, political, cultural. This even applies to Tennyson, in many ways the most orthodox of them all. Tennyson had himself used trochaic octameters in 'Locksley Hall', the title poem of a volume which, when it was published in 1842, brought him the fame that Browning hoped to achieve with *Men and Women.* It may even be that there is a hint of competitiveness in 'A Toccata'. 'Locksley Hall' was written in couplets. Browning's verses are triplets. Going one better, it might be thought.

But then it has also to be noted that in her volume of 1844, Elizabeth Barrett includes a poem called 'Lady Geraldine's Courtship', which uses trochaic octameters in quatrain stanzas:

> Dear my friend and fellow-student, I would lean my spirit
> o'er you!
> Down the purple of this chamber tears should scarcely run
> at will.
> I am humbled who was humble. Friend, I bow my head
> before you:
> You should lead me to my peasants, but their faces are too
> still.

Others who used the metre include Thackeray and William Jeffry Prowse, about whom we know nothing except that he is the author of the beautiful elegy on the great cricketer, Alfred Mynn, the last stanza of which runs:

> All were proud of him, all loved him. As the changing
>   seasons pass,
> As our champion lies asleeping underneath the Kentish
>   grass,
> Proudly, sadly we will name him – to forget him were a sin.
> Lightly lie the turf upon thee, kind and manly Alfred Mynn.

And Hardy's 'Friends Beyond' characteristically exploits the form by introducing a short middle line between the octameter couplets:

> William Dewy, Tranter Reuben, Farmer Ledlow late at
>   plough,
>   Robert's kin, and John's, and Ned's,
> And the Squire, and Lady Susan, lie in Mellstock
>   churchyard now!

The long line has always been a preoccupation with English poets. It *ought* to be possible to push beyond the pentameter, but Tudor and Elizabethan attempts at fourteeners and poulter's measure (alternating lines of twelve and thirteen feet, and thus a term of contempt for poulterers, who couldn't count properly) had by and large failed; and until Arthur Hugh Clough's brilliant handling of the hexameter, in *The Bothie of Tober-na-Vuolich* (1848) and *Amours de Voyage* (1849), nobody had been able to sustain six-stress lines over more than a short stretch. Clough was a contemporary of Tennyson and Browning, a political, radical and religious sceptic; and like them, his formal experiments imply a deep dissatisfaction with those orthodoxies which Matthew Arnold spoke for when he criticised his friend's rejection of "lyricism" and "beauty". Why, Arnold wanted to know, was Clough so determined to break up the formal perfections of lyric poetry? The answer of course is that Clough saw in such perfection an enacted lie, a pretence that God's in his heaven, all's right with the world.

This brings us back to Browning. For the eponymous heroine of his verse play, *Pippa Passes* (1841) sings those very words as she goes about her day's tasks, innocently doing good. She is not however to be thought of as speaking with her author's voice. No more is the speaker of 'A Toccata of Galuppi's'. "I was never out of England" – by the time Browning has his protagonist say this, he himself was in Italy, with his much-loved wife and intellectual companion. Still, he shares with that protagonist a passion for music. Browning played both piano and organ, and in 1847 a visitor to the Brownings in Florence reported that he and the poet walked to a nearby convent chapel where "Browning at the organ chased a fugue, or dreamed out upon the twilight keys a faint throbbing toccata of Galuppi's". Whether this is true or not – and there seems no good reason to doubt it – Galuppi was undoubtedly a composer Browning admired. At one time he had in his possession two huge manuscript volumes almost exclusively made up of Galuppi's "Toccata-pieces". So less than flattering references in the poem to Galuppi's "cold music" must not be misunderstood. It is not Galuppi who is being criticised, but the man who speaks. Or rather, the mid-19th century amateur musician can find no comfort in the work of an 18th century Venetian composer. That being said, who was Galuppi?

The short answer is that Baldassare Galuppi, 1706-1785, was and is still known mainly for light operas, although *Grove's Dictionary* remarks that "he had a firmer grasp of harmony, rhythm and orches-tration than most of his Italian contemporaries". Browning himself described a toccata as "apparently a slighter form of the Sonata to be 'touched' lightly off". It is entirely possible that Browning saw the composer as in a sense frustrated in his ambitions by the society that gave him work, never able to be as serious as he wanted to be, but, through his toccatas, able to make critical comment on the frivolity of Venetian life. Certainly the man who plays the toccata and muses on it as he plays seems to think this. And yet, because on his own admission he was "never out of England", it may be that the Venice he conjures up is little more than a huddle of clichés. "But although I take your meaning, 'tis with such a heavy mind." The "meaning" turns out to be that "they lived once thus". *How* the Venetians lived is then imagined in terms of ball and masquerade, flirtation, sexual peccadillo:

What? Those lesser thirds so plaintive, sixths diminished,
    sigh on sigh,
– Told them something? Those suspensions, those solutions
    – 'Must we die?'
Those commiserating sevenths – 'Life might last! We can
    but try!'

'Were you happy? – 'Yes.' – 'And are you still as happy?'
    – 'Yes. And you?'
– 'Then, more kisses!' – 'Did *I* stop them, when a million
    seemed so few?'
Hark, the dominant's persistence till it must be answered
    to!

So, an octave struck the answer.

The technical skill of this writing is of the highest order. I know of
no other poet in the language – Hardy not excepted – who can so
naturally blend voices into the demands of metre as to produce
dialogue that is full of what Robert Frost demanded of true poetry –
"sentence sound". (You have only to glance at the movement of
speech in 'Locksley Hall' to recognise that Browning's handling of
dialogue is far more supple than Tennyson's.)

But the reading of Venice derived from the music is not necessarily
Browning's. The man who plays Galuppi's toccata and finds in it a
meaning he thinks he can't misconceive is, after all, limited to a
'knowledge' that was common among northerners, especially the
English. Broadly speaking, Venice was 'known' to be a place of
infamy. It was Byron, of course, who had done more than anyone to
give it that especial reputation; and it hung on until long after the
publication of Browning's poem. But what is fascinating about the
speaker of the poem is that he's not so much shocked as intrigued,
obsessed we might almost say, by the Venice he thinks Galuppi's
music uncovers for him. And it is here that matters become more
complicated.

"Those commiserating sevenths", "the dominant's persistence",
"So, an octave struck the answer". The technical language is clearly
of great importance. According to an authority on Venetian music,
Dr Victor Crowther, "one of Vivaldi's favourite formulae (copied by
other Venetians) for extending the life of his instrumental pieces

(Browning's 'Life might last!') was to treat a musical phrase sequentially, underpinning it with harmony moving methodically down the circle/spiral of fifths by way of interlocking seventh-chord ... By these means, the 'suspensions' mentioned in the previous line of the poem are given a longer lease of life; resolution (death) is delayed." As to the dominant: "In 1750 a long dominant pedal-point was a stock device for signalling a return to the home key (tonic) at the end of a piece." And Crowther also points out that the "octave", quite apart from implying the tonic, has religious overtones. It embodies that ultimate harmony which is God-ordained, is in fact symbolic of the harmonious universe.

The answer that the octave brings ought, then, to bring satisfaction along with it. That it doesn't is obvious from the tone of the poem's concluding stanzas. Instead, deep regret, an aching sense of loss, is surely what throbs through them? And this is odd for a number of reasons. In the first place, it denies the power of music's resolving harmonies. Or rather, it suggests that such harmonies bring discomfort rather than consolation. In the second place, this feeling of discomfort is a long way from the kind of moral fervour customarily shining through performances of classical music that found favour in mid-19th century England. (Handel's *Messiah* and Mendelssohn's oratorios were thought to be especially uplifting.) It was no doubt for this reason that Ernest Walker, in his *History of Music in England* (1907) remarked on the poor quality of the nation's religious music and concluded: "it is only in England that musicianship has been really seriously hampered by the unmusical seekers after edification." And this, then, alerts us to the fact that for the man at the piano to have chosen Galuppi's music at all is a mark of extreme eccentricity. It hints at a desire to eat forbidden fruit.

That this is indeed so can be inferred from the ardency with which the musician dreams himself into that warm Venetian world of his imagination. We are beyond the platitudes of stock response here, though it undoubtedly starts from them:

> Was a lady such a lady, cheeks so round and lips so red, –
> On her neck the small face buoyant, like a bell-flower on its
>   bed,
> O'er the breast's superb abundance where a man might
>   base his head?

Not in England, he mightn't. But this world is, according to the musician's interpretation of Galuppi, shallow, bound for death. The cold music tells him:

> 'Dust and ashes, dead and done with, Venice spent what Venice earned.
> The soul, doubtless, is immortal – where a soul can be discerned.
>
> 'Yours for instance: you know physics, something of geology,
> Mathematics are your pastime; souls shall rise in their degree;
> Butterflies may dread extinction, – you'll not die, it cannot be!

And here, suddenly, we have the explanation for the poem's mixture of almost voyeuristic sensuality, sadness, and deep, blank regret. For it is precisely because he's a scientist that this amateur musician has every cause to dread extinction. What physics, geology and mathematics were alike discovering in the years immediately prior to the publication of the poem was that the account of the origins of the universe as taught by the Church made no sense. Lyell's *Principles of Geology*, Chambers' *Vestiges of Creation*, the papers which Darwin had published as a result of his voyages on HMS *Beagle* and much else beside – what were these but irrefutable-seeming denials of the proposition that "souls shall rise in their degree"?

This is why the poem ends with that extraordinary, plangent note in which are combined a final glance at the golden world from which the speaker feels himself to be shut out, and the utterance of someone close to despair:

> 'Dust and ashes.' So you creak it, and I want the heart to scold.
> Dear dead women, with such hair, too – what's become of all the gold
> Used to hang and brush their bosoms? I feel chilly and grown old.

"I want the heart to scold." Meaning, I lack the heart to scold the women. Why *shouldn't* they have lived their lives the way they chose to? And, just possibly, we can read the phrase as meaning: I wish I had the heart to scold you, Galuppi. At all events, the music's confidence is, we now know, misplaced. The dominant's persistence may have signalled death, but it couldn't symbolise a world of universal harmony in which God, the mathematician, established for ever the grounds of concord, of regularity. There *is* no such harmony. What then, was wrong with the lives the Venetian people chose to lead? The question, or one very like it, underlies much mid-19th century humanist thought. Hence, George Eliot's resolute and, some might say, desperate pronouncement about God, immortality and duty: how inconceivable the one, how impossible the second, yet how absolute and peremptory the third. It is not a peremptoriness that the speaker of Browning's poem can be at ease with. "I feel chilly and grown old." The penultimate stress is thrown forward to give the effect of a spondee: grówn óld. As though he has had no youth, and, in Larkin's famous words, can now contemplate merely age and then only the end of age.

From which we may conclude that the speaker isn't in fact old, but that he feels himself to have missed out on life, or as much of it as is contained in Galuppi's dismissive account of its "mirth and folly". Yet if this is so, the poem can be read as deeply, and therefore hearteningly, subversive. Its relish for sexual love, for the life of the senses, for appetency – this is surely to be preferred to those conformities with which the poem's protagonist has, so it feels, been forced to abide. (What he imagines Galluppi dismissing as mere mirth and folly could, after all, be seen in an altogether more affirmative manner.) It follows that, far from being a necessary cause of moral and metaphysical anguish, of unwilled disillusionment with the 'truths' of revealed religion, scientific truths may be liberating. This is not to say they have proved so for the man who speaks Browning's poem. For him, their bleak finality cancels the value of his life without offering him the chance of any other, and it would be absurd to deny the authenticity of his pain. But it *is* to say that for the men and women who read 'A Toccata of Galuppi's' in 1855 (and later?), a world born "to bloom and drop", when imagined by less timorous or orthodox minds, could become a world of releasing possibilities.

Not that these are explored in the poem that follows. 'By the

Fire-Side', which I take Browning to have deliberately positioned immediately after the 'Toccata', is a tribute to domestic warmth and companionship. It is also about a true love relationship. Unlike the speaker of the previous poem, who feels "chilly and grown old", the speaker of 'By the Fire-Side' is warmed by the knowledge of shared intellectual and physical passion. His house is blest by the *lares* and *penates*, those Roman gods of the household that bring with them warmth and hospitality. It's therefore with no sense of smugness that the speaker can address his wife and companion, can say to her:

> I will speak now,
> No longer watch you as you sit
> Reading by the fire-light, that great brow
> And the spirit-small hand propping it,
> Mutely, my heart knows how –
>
> When, if I think but deep enough,
> You are wont to answer, prompt as rhyme;
> And you, too, find without rebuff
> Response your soul seeks many a time
> Piercing its fine flesh-stuff.
>
> (stanzas xxiii-xxiv)

Out of context this may perhaps seem either uxorious or presumptuous: a show of husbandly devotion or a claim to knowledge he can't possibly have. But the tone of voice is so secure in its intimate musing that it is stamped with its own guarantee. For while the poem unwinds an intricate web of connected thoughts between present and past and in so doing tells us much about the habit of mind of the speaker, it is above all a tribute to the loved woman:

> If two lives join, there is oft a scar,
> They are one and one, with a shadowy third;
> One near one is too far.
>
> A moment after, and hands unseen
> Were hanging the night around us fast;
> But we knew that a bar was broken between
> Life and life: we were mixed at last
> In spite of the mortal screen.
>
> (stanzas xivi-ivii)

Given that he adds a few stanzas later "So grew my own small life complete,/ As nature obtained her best of me –/ One born to love you, sweet", we might want to see in this love relationship yet another instance of elective affinity. There is however a difference. This particular relationship is as much one of intellectual companionship as it is of physical passion, and while an elective affinity makes bold to assert a complete merging of identities – "Nellie, I *am* Heathcliff" is more resonant than "One near one is too far" but otherwise seems to be very much the same kind of statement – it allows little scope for the confident, confiding tone of this poem, one that is characterised by such affectionate gratitude that at the end it even permits the speaker to make a whimsical joke:

> So, earth has gained by one man the more,
>> And the gain of earth must be heaven's gain too;
> And the whole is well worth thinking o'er
>> When autumn comes: which I mean to do
> One day, as I said before.

You come round the end of the penultimate line and find that resolve – "which I mean to do" – is after all deferred. "One day". It's a hint, self-deprecating but nevertheless unmissable, of his determination to be his own man for all their closeness. Yet the poem has in fact been engaged with exactly the "thinking o'er" the speaker apparently disowns. 'By the Fire-Side' ends on exactly the right note: wry, humorous, tender, graceful in its acknowledgement of the wife's unrivalled importance in the life of "one man", above all *intimate*.

In his essay, 'The Three Voices of Poetry', T.S. Eliot worries away at the difficulty of writing love poetry. "My opinion is", Eliot says, "that a good love poem, though it may be addressed to one person, is always meant to be overheard by other people. Surely the proper language of love – that is, of communication to the beloved and to no one else – is prose." He may have had in mind the embarrassment caused by writers who insist on going public over their love affairs. When D.H. Lawrence wrote a sequence of love poems about his marriage to Frieda he gave it the title, *Look, We Have Come Through*. "They may have come through," Bertrand Russell rejoined, "but why should I look?" The reason to look at 'By the Fire-Side' is because it is an exemplary poem of married love. Most love poems are about pre- or non-married love. Louis MacNeice's sardonic 'Les Sylphides' is to the point here. His two ardent lovers

> were married – to be the more together –
> And found they were never again so much together,
> Divided by the morning tea,
> By the evening paper,
> By children and tradesmen's bills.

Seven years after Browning published *Men and Women*, George Meredith's sonnet sequence, *Modern Love*, anatomised with ruthless brilliance a marriage in which neither partner finds any satisfaction, except, perversely, in hurting the other. Yet Browning's poem can with justification be thought of as equally modern, simply because the woman's equal (perhaps superior) intellect is taken for granted. To be sure, Tennyson had already treated, though with some unease, the matter of women's education in *The Princess*, (1847). The Prince of this poem, intended as an enlightened male, may say that

> in true marriage lies
> Nor equal, nor unequal: each fulfils
> Defect in each, and always thought in thought,
> Purpose in purpose, will in will they grow,
> The single pure and perfect animal ...

but his claim lacks substance because we never see the "true marriage" of which he speaks. Nor can we find it in *David Copperfield*, (1851), for all that Dickens so acutely explores the cost of unequal marriages, so wonderfully fleshes out the cry of one of the novel's female characters, that "there can be no disparity in marriage like the unsuitability of mind and purpose." As it is easier to make evil more interesting than good, so it is easier to write about unhappy marriages than happy ones. To adapt Tolstoy's famous remark at the beginning of *Anna Karenina*, "all happy marriages are more or less like one another; every unhappy marriage is unhappy in its own particular way." This is what makes 'By the Fire-Side' so rare an achievement, in every sense of the word rare. And that Browning knew as much is evident from 'Two in the Campagna'. In this poem a rather pompous young man bellyaches that his lover isn't his equal, or he hers, or that anyway they don't seem to have struck the perfect match he'd promised himself. "I would that you were all to me,/ You that are just so much, no more." It's a good enough rendering of male dissatisfaction ("it isn't my fault") blended into complacent introspectiveness, (with its implied "gosh, aren't I interesting") but it's nowhere near the level of 'By the Fire-Side'.

As to 'Childe Roland to the Dark Tower Came', this *tour de force* is quite unlike anything else in Browning or, for that matter, in English poetry as a whole. I suspect Browning himself didn't quite know what to do with it – it is sandwiched rather awkwardly between the inconsiderable 'A Pretty Woman' and 'Respectability' – but knew, too, that the poem was the luck that can come to any poet perhaps once in a life time. (As 'The Rhyme of the Ancient Mariner' came to Coleridge, leaving him, T.S. Eliot thought, ever afterwards a haunted man.). On different occasions Browning, when interrogated about his poem's meaning, said that it came to him as "a kind of dream", that he had no idea what it meant, and that it was a "fantasy" without allegoric intent. However, when someone asked him whether the poem might mean that "he that endureth to the end shall be saved", he answered "Just about that." I doubt it.

But then so much in the poem is slippery with doubt that it seems endlessly to elude our understanding, and this, though 'Childe Roland' is one of the most graphic poems Browning ever wrote. You could hardly ask for anything more vivid than the opening stanza:

> My first thought was, he lied in every word,
>> That hoary cripple, with malicious eye
>> Askance to watch the working of his lie
> On mine, and mouth scarce able to afford
> Suppression of the glee, that pursed and scored
>> Its edge, at one more victim gained thereby.

This could be the opening of a tale about the quest to find the Castle Perilous, and in a sense it is. But in the traditional quest tale there is always a clear end in view, and the arrival at the Castle (or for that matter the grasping of the Grail) is a reward for virtues shown during the quest itself: courage, endurance, singleness of purpose – that is, resistance to any allure that might lead you from the true path. (The temptation is usually represented as a seductive woman.) Christian literature has many Quest heroes, including such notables as Parsifal (the holy fool who rescues the grail from the wicked magician, Klingsor), the Red Cross Knight (of Spenser's *Faerie Queene*), and Bunyan's hero, the aptly named Christian. And though quest literature may have its origin in classical tales such as the twelve labours of Hercules or, at a pinch, Jason's pursuit of the fleece, there is a significant difference. Hercules isn't motivated by regard for his virtue or promise of a life beyond the grave, and Jason is positively wimpish. He not only bursts into tears on occasions when he thinks Fortune is against him, but he lets Medea do the really dangerous work of capturing the Fleece. In steep contrast, the famous poem (later to become a hymn) that Valiant recites towards the close of *Pilgrim's Progress* is clear indication of how Bunyan regards the true Christian hero:

> There's no discouragement
> Shall make him once relent
> His first avowed intent
>   To be a pilgrim.
>
> Who so beset him round
>   With dismal stories,
> Do but themselves confound,
>   His strength the more is:
> No lion can him fright:
> He'll with a giant fight ...
>
> Hobgoblin nor foul fiend
>   Can daunt his spirit:
> He knows he at the end
> Shall life inherit ...

And there's the rub. The full title of Bunyan's great work is *The Pilgrim's Progress From This World to That Which Is To Come*. The reward for proving yourself a true Pilgrim is arrival at the celestial city, at the gate of which stand "trumpeters and pipers; with singers and players on stringed instruments – to welcome the pilgrims as they went up, and followed one another in at that beautiful gate of the city."

In his Dictionary, Johnson defined a pilgrim as "a traveller, a wanderer; particularly one who travels on a religious account." He also defined wandering as having "always an ill meaning". Wandering signified lawlessness in the literal sense that a wanderer was outside or beyond the law. Gipsys are wanderers. The word could also signify madness. (We still speak of people whose minds 'wander'.) And Johnson, solidly Tory, thought men should always live within the law and distrust flights of fancy. Flight was a form of lawless travel, whether it meant fleeing – you customarily fled the law – or space travel, which was reserved for angels and devils, and men couldn't be angels. Johnson was temperamentally disinclined to enthuse over heroism. Heroism was dangerous, hero-worship worse. Better by far to cultivate your own garden than go in pursuit of glory, even Christian glory. Better in other words to keep within the law than risk transgressing it. But of course the compulsion that drives a Christian to be a pilgrim often requires him to deny or break the law of the land. Bunyan spent long years in prison for daring to preach his gospel. And Bunyan was a wandering tinker. Until quite recently, 'tinker' was a term of abuse directed at those who flouted the law or respectability. Now, there are no tinkers.

How does this help us with Browning's poem, which begins with his unnamed protagonist – a knight on horseback? – turning off the public way in response to the cripple who, he assumes, is set to "waylay with his lies, ensnare/ All travellers who might find him posted there,/ And ask the road"? In fact, it turns out that the cripple is telling the truth, is putting the rider on the right road. In Christian iconography, cripples, like beggars, are often gifted with the truth. So far, then, this might be a contemporary rewriting of an archetypal Christian quest poem. But the cripple's malicious eye, and his glee at the misfortune sure to come to one more seeker, are real enough. Moreover, the protagonist himself knows he is heading for failure:

> Thus, I had so long suffered in this quest,
>> Heard failure prophesied so oft, been writ
>> So many times among 'The Band' – to wit,
> The knights who to the Dark Tower's search addressed
> Their steps – that just to fail as they, seemed best,
>> And all the doubt was now – should I be fit?

(stanza vii)

Fit to fail? There is in Christian thinking a fine line between vaingloriousness and despair. ('Do not despair, one of the thieves was saved. Do not presume, one was crucified'). And it might be possible to imagine Browning's protagonist as guarding against hope. Yet at the end of the poem, when he arrives at the Tower, his ears are battered by a noise like a bell tolling names "Of all the lost adventurers my peers", and he sees them:

> To view the last of me, a living frame
> For one more picture! In a sheet of flame
> I saw them and I knew them all. And yet
> Dauntless the slug-horn to my lips I set,
>   And blew. '*Childe Roland to the Dark Tower Came.*'

If the Childe's peers compose "a living frame" this might mean that they have survived their ordeal. Yet the "sheet of flame" suggests that such survival is at best ambiguous, as though they have become part of a living hell. Even so, the phantasmogoric vision does not discourage him. "Dauntless" – bold, fearless, intrepid. A true Pilgrim.

But hardly a pilgrim of hope. Browning's poem might even be seen as a post-Christian quest, a Progress to the dark Tower of death or oblivion rather than the light of the celestial city. That Bunyan's work hovers somewhere behind 'Childe Roland' is obvious, as obvious as the fact that the waste, blasted landscape through which the pilgrim rides is one of despond. This is an unredeemed, pitiless land, of "starved ignoble nature", described with such remorseless accuracy as to send a shiver up any spine. "As for the grass, it grew as scant as hair/ In leprosy; thin dry blades pricked the mud/ Which underneath looked kneaded up with blood". "Glory be to God for dappled things", Hopkins was to write not many years later. Finding God in nature was a sustaining, salving practice for many 19th century writers at a time when God seemed to be withdrawing from the world, his footsteps no longer planted on the sea. The nature depicted in Browning's poem is entirely Godless. Either that, or it is imagined in Dantesque terms, as part of a hellishness beyond reach of mercy. "Drenched willows flung them headlong in a fit/ Of mute despair, a suicidal throng." Despair is the cardinal sin, suicide an act which places you beyond redemption. Such a landscape harbours death and horror. And so, when the rider crosses a river:

                                I feared
            To set my foot upon a dead man's cheek,
            Each step, or feel the spear I thrust to seek
         For hollows, tangled in his hair or beard!
         – It may have been a water-rat I speared,
                But ugh! It sounded like a baby's shriek.
                                (stanza xxi)

At the end of the decade in which Browning published his poem,
William Dyce painted 'Pegwell Bay, Kent, a recollection of 5th
October 1858'. The picture, which was completed in 1860 and now
hangs in the Tate Britain Gallery, shows women and children
collecting fossils from the beach below the bay's striated cliffs. It is
an unusually sombre picture, its mood, established by the low lighting
and the dark coloured clothes of the fossil-hunters, one of an almost
inexplicable sadness – until you take note of the picture's title, and
the date that Dyce gives as part of the title. This is about a nature
from which God has vanished. Geology had proved the world to be
far older than Christian account would have it. Darwin's *Origin of
Species* was published in 1859, and that Dyce should so carefully
date his picture to 1858 indicates that he wants viewers to understand
that they are looking from a disenchanted perspective back to a golden
time, are offered a last glimpse of a world over which a pall of sadness
has been thrown, now and for ever. Yet more than twenty years earlier
Charles Lyell, in his two-volume *Principles of Geology* (1830-1832)
had established the scientific procedures by which to date the earth's
formation, as a result of which it became impossible to sustain the
Christian belief that God had created the world in seven days, let
alone that he had brought it into existence four thousand years before
the birth of Christ, as the Church taught. Ruskin wasn't the only
19th century person to hear the clink of the geologist's hammer at
the end of each verse of the Bible, its metallic sound mocking the
words of God's purpose for his chosen universe.

   The title of Browning's poem is also important. Under 'Childe
Roland to the Dark Tower Came', the poet adds in brackets "See
Edgar's song in Lear." What Edgar, by now disguised as Mad Tom,
actually sings in Act 3 scene iv of Shakespeare's play is not so much
a song as a fragment:

Childe Rowland to the Dark Tower came.
His word was still 'Fie, foh, and fum',
I smell the blood of a British man.

There has been endless editorial speculation about these mysterious lines. All agree that Childe Rowland must be here a reference to Orlando, and that 'Childe' was a term regularly given to young men who were candidates for knighthood. To become a knight entails the completion of some test or tests, a feat of strength, endurance, and so on. The *Chanson de Roland*, one of the most famous of all medieval Romances – it was probably composed sometime during the 11th century – is about Charlemagne's nephew, Orlando, who dies an heroic death in a foreign land. The fragment of song Edgar sings begins with a reference to the *Chanson*. But then comes a problem. Why on earth should Roland use words that are traditionally spoken by the Giant of a long-famous ballad, 'Jack and the Giants'? Some editors have suggested that a line from Edgar's song has gone missing, and that we have to imagine a giant emerging from the Dark Tower to utter the words. Others suggest that in his distress Edgar thinks that his father, who is present at the scene, has penetrated his disguise and recognised beneath 'Mad Tom's' rags a true British man. All are agreed that the lines suggest a fearful opposition between the Childe and whatever principle or force emanates from the Dark Tower itself.

My tentative suggestion is that for Browning the Childe represents the spirit of Quest, while the Tower represents or symbolises or in some way embodies a godless universe, one without light or redemptive purpose. The Childe's quest is therefore bound to end in defeat. And I will add that a possible sub-meaning is that this world of strenuous quest is very noticeably an exclusively male one. It is significant that as the rider journeys alone through the wasteland – this being no last ride together – his mind roves back to two companions, questers who came to bad ends. One, Giles, was a traitor to the cause, although we aren't told how he became so. His defection may have been to a more normative world. We can't know this, of course, but we can be sure that the other questor lost his way through "one night's disgrace." Cuthbert, we infer, went wrong because of a woman. This killed off the friendship between him and the Childe. "Out went my heart's new fire and left it cold." If we then think back to 'Respectability' and 'A Light Woman', we may want to read the quest undertaken in 'Childe Roland' as intrinsically flawed. The "need of a world of men" leads to the phallocentric dark tower that presides over a cursed, sterile landscape.

III

That at least one of Browning's contemporaries thought the poet was likely to find Christian apologetics ultimately unsatisfactory is evident from George Eliot's account of 'Bishop Blougram's Apology'. The Bishop, she says, is:

> ... bent on proving by the most exasperatingly ingenious sophistry, that the theory of life on which he grounds his choice of being a bishop, though a doubting one, is wiser in the moderation of its ideal, with the certainty of attainment, than the Gigadibs theory, which aspires after the highest and attains nothing. The way in which Blougram's motives are dug up from below the roots, and laid bare to the very last fibre, not by a process of hostile exposure, not by invective or sarcasm, but by making himself exhibit them with a self-complacent sense of supreme acuteness, and even with a crushing force of worldly common sense, has the effect of masterly satire.

George Eliot's account appeared in the *Westminster Review* in January 1856, and I quote it, partly to show that not all of Browning's first critics were blind to his great powers, but because as an agnostic herself George Eliot takes a view of the poem that is markedly less hostile to the Bishop than most later commentators have been. Here, then, we must note that the word 'Apology' has a dual meaning. It is a regret for error, but it can also mean self-justification. Hence, to name one famous 19th century example, Cardinal John Henry Newman's *Apologia Pro Vita Sua* (1865). We should also note that while it may be difficult to take Bishop Blougram's apology for his way of life at face value, it is even more difficult to take seriously anyone called Gigadibs, (a gig is, among other things, a light horse-driven vehicle, a whipping-top and a frivolous girl), and this particular man is an entirely lightweight character. Browning himself felt he had treated Blougram "not ungenerously", which fainthearted endorsement fairly suggests his disinterested approach to the argument between the two men about how best to live your life.

In his still persuasive pages on the poem, Robert Langbaum shrewdly notes that the Bishop "cannot convert Gigadibs because his argument, for all its suggestion of a Truth higher than itself, must be understood dramatically as rationalising a selfish worldly existence. What Gigadibs apparently does learn is that he is no better than the bishop ... and that he has been as intellectually and morally dishonest with his sentimental liberalism as the bishop with his casuistry." This is well said and alerts us to one of Browning's greatest strengths: his endless, restless desire to put all ideas to the test, never to find contentment with any one position. Scott Fitzgerald said that the test of a first-rate intelligence is its ability to hold contradictory ideas and still retain the capacity to function. Browning's poetry is built on contradiction: within and between poems. Assertion is met by counter-assertion, certainty by question and, sometimes, denial. Even "How it Strikes A Contemporary", an account of a poet that many have felt comes as close as Browning ever did to providing his own apologia, cannot quite be taken on trust. For characteristically, we see this poet from glimpses provided by an outsider who at the very outset says "I only knew one poet in my life".

Nevertheless, the account of this (unnamed) poet suggests he is an exemplar of that negative capability Keats thought essential to poetic creativity. Keats' explanation for this phrase comes in a letter to his brothers, written at the tail end of 1817. Negative Capability, he tells them, underlining the phrase, "is when a man is capable of being in uncertainties, mysteries, doubts, without any irritable reaching after fact and reason." Shakespeare is the supreme example. In October of the following year, in a letter to his friend Richard Woodhouse, he developed the idea, although by then he had dropped the actual phrase. He is here trying to define what he takes to be the "poetical character":

> I mean that sort, of which if I am anything, I am a member;
> (that sort distinguished from the Wordsworthian, or egotistical
> Sublime; which is a thing per se, and stands alone), it is not
> itself – it has no self. It is every thing and nothing – It has no
> character – it enjoys light and shade; it lives in gusto, be it
> foul or fair, high or low, rich or poor, mean or elevated. – It
> has as much delight in conceiving an Iago as an Imogen. What
> shocks the virtuous philosopher delights the chameleon poet.

> It does no harm from its relish of the dark side of things, any more than from its taste for the bright one, because they both end in speculation. A poet is the most unpoetical of anything in existence, because he has no Identity – he is continually in for and filling some other body.

Gusto and relish: words that could perfectly well be applied to Browning. And the poet described in 'How It Strikes a Contemporary' answers very well to the Keatsian imperatives for the poetical character. For this poet enters sympathetically into all lives presented to him:

> He stood and watched the cobbler at his trade,
> The man who slices lemons into drink,
> The coffee-roaster's brazier, and the boys
> That volunteer to help him turn its winch ...
> He took such cognisance of men and things,
> If any beat a horse, you felt he saw;
> If any cursed a woman, he took note ...
> We had among us, not so much a spy,
> As a recording chief-inquisitor,
> The town's true master, if the town but knew.

To this end, the poet is as it were in mufti, not seeking the bright lights, nor making himself a darling of high society, nor treating himself as flaunting his status, with "twenty naked girls to change his plate." Rather, to all outer appearance, he is anonymous "Playing a decent cribbage with his maid", his life an unremarkable routine. "Nine,/Ten, struck the church clock, straight to bed went he." Reading those lines I think of the poet Peter Porter's characteristically witty remark that there is "no unanimity of poetical signs. Even beautiful, haunted, poetical young men may turn out to be poets."

But they may also lose the plot, become snared by the attraction of fame, money, beautiful women. This is the lesson of the master. It is also the subject of 'Andrea del Sarto' (called 'The Faultless Painter'). This great poem comes immediately after a short lyric, 'Memorabilia', which begins:

> Ah, did you once see Shelley plain,
>   And did he stop and speak to you

> And did you speak to him again?
> How strange it seems and new!

Shelley is a true poetic hero, a spirit uncontaminated by worldly hopes or lures of the flesh. (So Browning thought at the time, although when he later found out about Shelley's tangled love affairs and less than honourable dealing with his first wife he became disenchanted with the great Sun-treader.) The four-stanza poem ends with the speaker putting inside his breast "a moulted feather, an eagle-feather!". Shelley is a true king among artists, unlike the man who claims eagle status for himself in 'A Light Woman'.

And unlike Andrea del Sarto. There has been a good deal of discussion about whether Browning was unfair to the actual 16th century artist, details of whose life he took from Vasari. But this is hardly to the point. Browning's interest is in the kind of sad self-loathing of a man who knows he has failed his own sense of high calling, of devotion to the responsibility of being a true artist. Browning does not satirise the speaker of this poem. The painter is never complacent or self-deceiving, as is the case with both the Bishops of those other great dramatic monologues on which I have commented. What makes Andrea del Sarto a sympathetic character is that he knows all too well how greatly he has failed, but must keep the knowledge from his wife, for whom he has given up much in order to ensure her continued love. As so often with Browning, the poem starts in medias res: it's as though a door swings open and we find ourselves the evesdroppers on an ongoing speech, in this case the pleading words of husband to wife:

> But do not let us quarrel any more,
> No, my Lucrezia; bear with me for once:
> Sit down and all shall happen as you wish.
> You turn your face, but does it bring your heart?
> I'll work then for your friend's friend, never fear,
> Treat his own subject after his own way,
> Fix his own time, accept too his own price,
> And shut the money into this small hand
> When next it takes mine. Will it? Tenderly?

Reading this I find it impossible not to think of George Eliot's study of the relationship between Lydgate and Rosamund Vincy in

Middlemarch. Lydgate, the great doctor-to-be, ends up treating fashionable patients, making a great deal of money for his wife to spend, and carrying to his grave the knowledge of how he failed himself. George Eliot is sympathetic to Lydgate but also accuses him of "spots of commonness" – in particular his love of pretty women and his readiness to be flattered by their attentions. Something of the same seems to be true of Browning's artist. And like Lydgate he knows the full extent of his failure but cannot share this with his wife. For she is at least partly the cause of that failure. At one point, speaking of others who strive to paint well, he says:

> There burns a truer light of God in them,
> In their vexed beating stuffed and stopped-up brain,
> Heart, or whate'er else, than goes on to prompt
> This low-pulsed forthright craftsman's hand of mine.
> Their work drops groundward, but themselves, I know,
> Reach many a time a heaven that's shut to me ...
>
> (lls 79-85)

Andrea is another Lost Leader, although Browning does not treat him with scorn, and there is no doubting the intensity of his love for his wife. "You called me, and I came home to your heart./ The triumph was – to reach and stay there; since/ I reached it ere the triumph, what is lost?" The answer of course is, everything. In gaining the world of respectability, of gold and social position, he has willingly surrendered the claims of true art. This could be a proleptic account of the career of many English artists of Browning's or any other time. It is certainly a great, wise, sad poem.

When Browning was old and belatedly famous, and a regular diner-out, Henry James was, as we have seen, bewildered to distraction by the poet's affable, shallow conversations, his bland public appearance. Where was the great poet, James wanted to know? The answer is, in the pages of *Men and Women*.

5   *Dramatis Personae*

A year after the appearance of *Men and Women* Elizabeth Barrett Browning published *Aurora Leigh*, a long, book-length poem which rightly earned her high praise and made her, after Tennyson, the most famous poet of the mid-century. Ruskin described the poem as "the greatest *poem* in the language, unsurpassed by anything but Shakespeare – *not* surpassed by Shakespeare's *Sonnets*, and therefore the greatest poem in the language." Considering that *Aurora Leigh* is a poem much concerned with women's rights – the author herself remarked that with its publication she expected "to be put in the stocks ... as a disorderly woman and free-thinking poet" – Ruskin's praise must have raised an eyebrow or two, as it still does. For Ruskin would later go on to write 'Of Queen's Gardens', one of the two essays that make up *Sesame and Lilies*, (1864), his contribution to the ongoing debate about the respective roles of men and women in society. And there, Ruskin insists that it is a woman's duty to help her man. It is apparently Coriolanus' fault that he did not listen to his mother; it is Ophelia's that "she fails Hamlet at a critical moment." Moreover, while a girl should receive nearly the same education as a boy, there are differences of emphasis. "A man ought to know any language or science that he learns, thoroughly, while a woman ought to know the same language, or science, only so far as may enable her to sympathise in her husband's pleasures, and in those of his best friends."

Quite what the author of *Aurora Leigh* would have made of these words we cannot know – although it isn't difficult to guess. But by the time they appeared Elizabeth Barrett Browning had been for three years in her grave. After her death in Florence, on 29 June 1861, her husband moved himself and their young son, Pen, back to London, where he set up house. "I want my new life", he wrote at the time, "to resemble the last fifteen years as little as possible." There has been much speculation about the meaning of these words. Was Browning as good as admitting that married life had not been an especially pleasant experience, or was he saying that he couldn't bear anything that reminded him of his past happiness? Almost certainly, the latter. What *is* certain is that during his wife's lifetime

65

she had always been regarded as the major poet. And this may explain why, after the comparative failure of *Men and Women*, and even more after the huge success of *Aurora Leigh*, in which he genuinely delighted, Browning wrote very little.

Until, that is, the return to England. Then, quite suddenly, he began once more to produce poems. By 1864 he had enough for a further hefty collection, and in that year he published *Dramatis Personae*. It was the first book to bring him anything like popular success. The first edition quickly sold out and before the end of the year a second, revised, edition was on the bookstalls. By previous standards this was a considerable achievement, though not one we should over-estimate. Browning's publishers, Chapman and Hall, still had over 500 unsold copies of the second edition on their hands in 1868. Nevertheless, he was now beginning to be recognised as a major poet. And poems such as 'James Lee's Wife', 'Abt Vogler', 'Rabbi Ben Ezra', 'Caliban upon Setebos' and 'Mr Sludge, "The Medium"', were much admired.

Rightly so. They are all important works. Yet both individually and taken as a whole, the poems that make up *Dramatis Personae* do not mark an advance on *Men and Women*, which remains Browning's greatest achievement. That said, however, *Dramatis Personae* is a formidable achievement in its own right. Although, like its predecessor, it is certainly about men and women, there are important differences. Most significant, I think, is that the later volume is much more concerned with failure – and where not failure, disillusionment. And while I would never claim that we can read back from character to author (the title underlines the fact that the poems deal in invented characters) it seems fair to remark that Browning had no reason to expect *Dramatis Personae* to be any more successful than his previous books.

The first poem in the collection, 'James Lee's Wife' is in fact a sequence of poems about the failure of mutuality in marriage. In a letter to his friend Julia Wedgwood, written at the end of 1864, Browning said of the poem that he meant to depict a newly-married couple, "trying to realise a dream of being sufficient to each other, in a foreign land (where you can try such an experiment) and finding it break up – the man being tired *first*, – and tired precisely of the love." Perhaps the most arresting poem in the sequence is the second, called 'By the Fireside', the title inevitably recalling the wonderful lyric meditation *of Men and Women*, although there a man speaks, while here it is the wife who muses over her life on "this bitter coast of France":

> God help you, sailors, at your need!
>> Spare the curse!
> For some ships, safe in port indeed,
>> Rot and rust,
>> Run to dust,
> All through worms i' the wood, which crept,
> Gnawed our hearts out while we slept:
>> That is worse.
>
> Who lived here before us two?
>> Old-world pairs.
> Did a woman ever – would I knew! –
>> Watch the man
>> With whom began
> Love's voyage full-sail, – (now, gnash your teeth)
> When planks start, open hell beneath
>> Unawares?
>>>>>>>> (stanzas iii and iv)

The bitterness of this is startling, although it wouldn't have been new to readers of the time. For as I mentioned earlier, Meredith had already produced his troubling anatomy lesson of *Modern Love*. In Browning's sequence of nine poems, as in Meredith's, we are given an almost claustrophobic sense of the couple, both inside and outside the house. But there comparisons end. The individual poems in 'James Lee's Wife' imply a progress from the first poem 'James Lee's Wife Speaks at the Window', through 'In the Doorway' – no. III, 'Along the Beach' – no. IV, to the final 'On Deck' – no. IX, about her sailing away from the wrecked marriage.

There is no such progress in *Modern Love*. I am dazzled by the technical accomplishment of 'James Lee's Wife', each individual poem written in different stanza form with its own, demanding, rhyme scheme. Perhaps the most perceptive of the poems' commentators is Patricia Ball, who, in *The Heart's Events*: *The Victorian Poetry of Relationships*, argues that Browning "is particularly acute in suggesting how experience is registered and passes into consciousness to become part of the recognised fabric of the self." As a result she suggests the poem as a whole shows him to be "both firmly pragmatic and deeply perceptive about relationships ... for the poem insists that human incompatibility and weakness, and the exigencies of 'seasonal' being, are facts to be accepted as the fuel of love even though they are undeniably elements which can dampen and extinguish its 'mutual flame'." Insofar as this (rightly) draws attention to Browning's scepticism about love as elective affinity, I agree. I worry only that the entire sequence doesn't so much develop an insight into the relationship between James Lee and his wife as admit to or betray a bafflement about what brought them together in the first place.

Years ago now, a student with whom I was discussing the poem put his finger on the problem, when he said, "why didn't she just leave him, for heaven's sake!" The obvious answer is that had she done so there would be no poem. And we ought to recognise and pay tribute to the great skill with which Browning has constructed what might be called the inner narrative of this failing marriage. We might also note that after an Act of 1857 divorce became a matter for the civil courts, although whereas a man could obtain a divorce if he proved his wife's adultery, for a woman the required grounds were her husband's cruelty, his adultery and/or 'unnatural practices', and what women was likely to go to court to prove such things? At least it can be said that Browning's exploration of a failing relationship in 'James Lee's Wife' is both enlightened and magnanimous.

'Abt Vogler', a very different kind of poem, springs from the poet's love of music and his expertise as an organist. More than that, Vogler (1749-1814) German composer, theorist, teacher, inventor of a musical instrument called an 'orchestrion', (a kind of large organ) and, as Browning's editors tell us, "noted extemporiser", had been "the master of John Relfe, Browning's music teacher." None of this can act as justification for a poem that at first glance may look to be one of those which explain why Browning was regarded with such bewildered head-shaking by his contemporaries. The subject of 'Abt Vogler' is of very great interest. The treatment feels initially bizarre. This, including its full title, is how it starts:

Abt Vogler
(After he has been extemporising upon the musical instrument of
his invention)

Would that the structure brave, the manifold music I build,
   Bidding my organ obey, calling its keys to their work,
Claiming each slave of the sound, at a touch, as when Solomon willed
   Armies of angels that soar, legions of demons that lurk,
Man, brute, reptile, fly, – alien of end and of aim,
   Adverse, each from the other heaven-high, hell-deep removed, –
Should rush into sight at once as he named the ineffable Name,
   And pile him a palace straight, to pleasure the princess he loved!

From this packed, bumpy cluster of words we can make out that as
with the man who plays a Toccato of Galuppi's, so Abt Vogler
imagines his music as able to construct a world – in his case an
"expression of the Absolute", which, in Langbaum's words, is "an
emanation from the soul's deepest wish." And, to quote Langbaum
again, this occurs in a poem that is "a dramatic monologue rather
than a philosophical statement, just to the extent that the statement
rises out of an illusion, out of a visual organisation of the world
limited in duration to the speaker's ecstatic moment of inspiration as
he extemporises on the organ." Abt Vogler certainly 'sees' a
harmonious universe achieved through his music:

And the emulous heaven yearned down, made efforts to reach the earth,
   As the earth had done her best, in my passion, to scale the sky:
Novel splendours burst forth, grew familiar, and dwelt with mine,
   Not a point nor peak but found and fixed its wandering star;
Meteor-moons, balls of blaze: and they did not pale nor pine,
   For earth had attained to heaven, there was no more near nor far.

I marvel at Browning's readiness to use a six-stress line here that
gives the lie to those who say that such a line can't be well handled
in English poetry. I admire quite as much the rapt, visionary exultation
with which Vogler imagines the universe's cosmic harmony, a kind
of Leibnizian affirmation of resolved purposes. I do, however, wish
there weren't so many awkward angles and crooks to negotiate, such
odd freaks of expression along the way. I can imagine the poem's
most determined apologist claiming that these rightly belong to the
character of Vogler himself, but this always seems a shade desperate,

a revisiting of the 'imitative fallacy' which should long ago have been laid to rest.

In the last of the poem's 11 stanzas Abt Vogler's vision fades. He comes down to earth, we might say. At all events, it's what he himself says:

> Well, it is earth with me; silence resumes her reign:
> > I will be patient and proud, and soberly acquiesce.
> Give me the keys. I feel for the common chord again,
> > Sliding by semitones, till I sink to the minor, – yes,
> And I blunt it into a ninth, and I stand on alien ground,
> > Surveying awhile the heights I rolled from into the deep;
> Which, hark, I have dared and done, for my resting-place is found,
> > The C Major of this life: so, now I will try to sleep.

This descent through the closing chords of his music, and the resolution through semitones to minor and then the silence that follows the last chord, repeats a key moment in 'A Toccato of Galuppi's' and, as there, transfers musical procedure to our common experience. The "common chord" is the C Major of mundane life, without sharps or flats. At the end of the poem Browning, no doubt deliberately, echoes the ending of Christopher Smart's 'Song to David' (1763), itself a great paean to God's universe:

> Glorious, – more glorious, is the crown
> Of Him that brought salvation down,
> > By meekness, called thy Son:
> Thou that stupendous truth believ'd; –
> And now the matchless deed's atchieved,
> > DETERMINED, DARED, and DONE.

Browning also echoes – perhaps unconsciously – the very last lines of Robert Bloomfield's *May Day With the Muses*, first published in 1822, which concludes with Bloomfield describing how a May Day's scenes of rural jollification gradually sink into night-time quiet. "The owl awoke, but dared not yet complain,/ And banish'd silence reassumed her reign." The echo is understandable in that Browning is writing about the gradual fading out of an ecstatic vision of cosmic harmony, much as Bloomfield had been writing about the darkening of a scene of rural harmony.

This brings me to a further point. In Bloomfield's poem the social harmony which *May Day With the Muses* celebrates belongs to the past. His poem is a kind of prolonged elegy for a vanishing way of life. Commentators on 'Abt Vogler' have suggested that the wondrous cosmic harmony which the musician glimpses as he plays is very much Browning's own. This may be because Browning himself chose the poem as one of four that he felt represented his work fairly. Yet the historical Abt Vogler was long dead by the time Browning wrote his poem. And as that poem was written after the appearance of *The Origin of Species*, it seems to me entirely proper to read it as celebrating a vision that can no longer be endorsed, very much as the amateur musician who plays Galuppi's Toccata looks back at a world of Christian belief from which as geologist he knows himself to be excluded.

If this is so, it will help to explain why Browning follows 'Abt Vogler' with 'Rabbi Ben Ezra':

> Grow old along with me!
> The best is yet to be,
> The last of life, for which the first was made:
> Our times are in his Hand
> Who saith 'A Whole I planned,
> Youth shows but half; trust God: see all nor be afraid!'

This is how the poem starts and reading it I can understand why some commentators have felt it introduces that image of Browning as virtually a caricature of the anti-intellectual poet perfectly summed up in Hardy's phrase about the "vulgar, dissenting grocer." Certainly Ben Ezra himself seems to breathe the kind of beery, cheery, scout-masterly outlook that gives optimism a bad name:

> Then, welcome each rebuff
> That turns earth's smoothness rough,
> Each sting that bids nor sit nor stand but go!
> Be our joys three-parts pain!
> Strive, and hold cheap the strain;
> Learn, nor account the pang; dare, never grudge the throe!
>
> (stanza vi)

"'Duty' was 'Nelson's watchword'", Samuel Smiles told his readers in *Self-Help*, that mid 19th century best seller. He might equally have chosen 'Striving'. "To strive, to seek, to find, and not to yield." This was what Tennyson's Ulysses told his companions should be their aim. "Say not the struggle naught availeth", Clough exhorted, more or less repeating the imploration of the Wily one. According to Pettigrew and Collins, "It is generally agreed that the Rabbi is a spokesman for Browning himself or for Browning as he would wish to be." They further tell us that the original Abraham Ibn Ezra (1092-1167), "a Spanish Jew, spent the latter half of his life travelling in exile; he was a most distinguished scholar and a man of genius in several areas." This may be so, but the poem itself makes little of those areas, preferring to show the Rabbi as a man of simple, unshakeable faith. At one point, indeed, he sounds as though he is taking up cudgels against the kind of worldly scepticism associated with, among others, Omar Khayyam. Edward Fitzgerald's *Rubaiyat* had been published in 1859 and although not at first a popular success – its fame came later – it is highly probable that Browning had read it. If so, he would have come across Omar's genial indifference to what he calls "the Quarrel of the Universe." Live for the day, he advises:

> And if the Wine you drink, the Lip you press,
> End in the Nothing all things end in – Yes –
>   Then fancy while Thou art, Thou art but what
> Thou shalt be – Nothing – Thou shalt not be less.
> While the Rose blows along the River Brink,
> With old Khayyam the vintage ruby drink …
> (stanzas xlviii-xlix)

The following words of Browning's Rabbi are surely meant as an answer to this philosophy of *carpe diem*:

>   Thou, to whom fools propound
>   When the wine makes its round,
> 'Since life fleets, all is change; the Past gone, seize today!'

>   Fool! All that is, at all,
>   Lasts ever, past recall;
> Earth changes, but thy soul and God stand sure
> (stanzas xxvi-xxvii)

As with 'Abt Vogler' so with 'Rabbi Ben Ezra': the voice that speaks with such confidence speaks from the past – in this case, a very remote one. And while its certainties may seem to rebuke the doubts, even genial cynicism of "old Khayyam", its own certainties are rebuked by subsequent scientific discoveries.

So, at least, I suggest, and I also suggest that the collection as a whole is eloquent of those doubts and uncertainties that so beset people in the latter half of the 19th century. Within *Dramatis Personae* itself there are poems suggesting that Browning's concern with failure, which as I say seems a leitmotif in the collection, is most acutely focused on a failure to prop up the claims for a God-given, purposive universe. This has an especial bearing on two key poems, 'Caliban Upon Setebos' and 'Mr Sludge, "The Medium"'.

Both of these have been so extensively discussed by Browning scholars and critics that it would be otiose to offer prolonged accounts of them here. Of the two, 'Caliban upon Setebos' is the more challenging, even difficult. It is also the more remarkable, *original*, and is without doubt the work of a very great poet. The poem's full title is 'Caliban upon Setebos: or, Natural Theology in the Island' and below it appears as epigraph 'Thou thoughtest that I was altogether such a one as thyself'. Natural theology does not depend on Revelation for its evidence as to God's existence, and such an existence was often argued for on natural grounds down to the 18th century – where, indeed, faith in "the best of all possible worlds" became a fashionable creed. Everything could be explained in the light of an ultimately benevolent purpose and this purpose was to be found in the world about you. The plenipotentiary universe was one where everything, even the least attractive or useful of phenomena, existed for good reason. Who needed deserts? Why, camels. But in the 19th century the claims of natural theology were put under the kind of stress not even Voltaire had imagined when, following the disaster of the Lisbon earthquake in which over 40,000 people died, he wrote his satire *Candide*, (1759) whose hapless protagonist, Pangloss, has an explanation for each and every misfortune. All is for the best in the best of all possible worlds.

Browning's Caliban is no Pangloss. He is not given to confident or complacent accounts of divine purpose. That he should speak of himself in the third person suggests moreover how far he is from self-knowledge, even further than is Shakespeare's half-man, half-monster. Philip Drew suggests that it is Caliban's terrible limitations that make him see God in his own image, cruel and vindictive. In saying this, Drew may have in mind the following lines:

> 'Saith He is terrible: watch His feats in proof!
> One hurricane will spoil six good months' hope.
> He hath a spite against me, that I know,
> Just as He favours Prosper, who knows why?
>
> (11s 200-3)

It is notable, however, that Caliban here talks about himself in the first person, as though he has come to some dreadful understanding of his own victimhood. Despite Drew's strictures, this seems to me perfectly reasonable. If after all the Church tells you that God is good and that, in the words of the harvest hymn, the fields are fed and watered "By God's almighty hand", and if you sing of how "He sends the warmth in winter" and the "soft, refreshing rain", then how *do* you explain the hurricane that ruins "six good months' hope"? Send for Pangloss? Or say with Cowper that:

> God moves in a mysterious way
> His wonders to perform,
> He plants his footsteps in the sea
> And rides upon the storm.

Cowper's great hymn, which he composed some time in the 1770s, at least acknowledges that God's divine purpose isn't easily discoverable by reference to the natural universe. But Caliban has no other point of reference.

This is a line pursued by Patricia Ball in the course of an essay in which she draws intriguing parallels between the universes of Browning and Samuel Beckett. She suggests that Caliban is a kind of tramp who settles down to wait for his Godot/Setebos. He is at once primitive and don, and this, she suggests, "is Browning's point about the human condition; and all his people, from Abt Vogler to Mr Sludge, illustrate it. Each constructs his Setebos, or his Quiet, each lives in accordance with his conception, each awaits confirmation of his own good, his own universe." On this reading,

Browning becomes one of those Honest Doubters – others include Matthew Arnold and Tennyson – who were so prevalent a feature of the 19th century, none able entirely to renounce the religious faiths with which they were nevertheless ill-at-ease. It was Tennyson who coined the phrase honest doubt, when, in 'In Memoriam', he wrote, "There lives more faith in honest doubt/ Believe me, than in half the creeds."

Caliban is not, it has to be said, an honest doubter. He is honestly, if clumsily, searching after the truth. And though his vision of divine purpose may be blurred, his vision of the near-at-hand is as sharp as Darwin himself could have wished. Anyone reading Darwin's *Voyage of the Beagle*, (1839) about his voyages in the south seas, will be aware of the extraordinary precision with which he describes the flora and fauna he encountered during his five years in and around South America. They will also be aware that Darwin is attentive to the fact that his observations bring him face to face with nature "red in tooth and claw", to quote Tennyson again. Here he is, for example, describing a fight to the death between a *Pepsis* wasp and a spider of the genus *Lycosa*:

> The wasp made a sudden dash at its prey, and then flew away: the spider was evidently wounded, for, trying to escape, it rolled down a little slope, but had still strength sufficient to crawl into a thick tuft of grass. The wasp soon returned, and seemed surprised at not immediately finding its victim. It then commenced as regular a hunt as ever hound did after fox; making short semicircular casts, and all the time rapidly vibrating its wings and antennae. The spider, though well concealed, was soon discovered; and the wasp, evidently still afraid of its adversary's jaws, after much manoeuvring, inflicted two stings on the underside of its thorax. At last, carefully examining with its antennae the now motionless spider, it proceeded to drag away the body.

Darwin reveals that he then intervened to drive the wasp off. It was this alertness to how nature works that did much to develop in him his theory about natural selection. Hence, his remark:

> We behold the face of nature bright with gladness, we often see superabundance of food; we do not see, or we forget, that

the birds which are idly singing round us mostly live on insects
or seeds, and are thus constantly destroying life; or we forget
how largely these songsters, or their eggs, or their nestlings,
are destroyed by birds and beasts of prey.

Caliban's vision is as sharp, his awareness of nature as disenchanted:

> Yon otter, sleek-wet, black, lithe as a leech;
> Yon auk, one fire-eye in a ball of foam,
> That floats and feeds; a certain badger brown
> He hath watched hunt with that slant white-wedge eye
> By moonlight; and the pie with the long tongue
> That pricks deep into oakwarts for a worm,
> And says a plain word when she finds her prize,
> But will not feed the ants ...
>
> (11s 46-53)

What makes 'Caliban upon Setebos' a great poem has much to do
with this extraordinary attentiveness to natural phenomena and
therefore a questioning of Divine Benevolence. As Shakespeare's
Caliban rejoices in the island's "sweet sounds, that give delight and
hurt not", so Browning's delights in the island's flora and fauna,
though acknowledging that they do hurt each other, as he hurts them
and God him:

> 'Thinketh, such shows nor right or wrong in Him,
> Nor kind, nor cruel: He is strong and Lord.
> 'Am strong myself compared to yonder crabs
> That march now from the mountain to the sea,
> 'Let twenty pass, and stone the twenty-first,
> Loving not, hating not, just choosing so.
> 'Say, the first straggler that boasts purple spots
> Shall join the file, one pincer twisted off;
> 'Say, this bruised fellow shall receive a worm,
> And two worms he whose nippers end in red;
> As it likes me each time, I do: so He.
>
> (11s 98-108)

The arbitrariness of fate may not be part of Darwin's thinking about
natural selection, but "Loving not, hating not, just choosing so" most

certainly is, and 'Caliban upon Setebos' is a great poem about trying to make sense of a world from which Divine Law seems to have vanished, leaving Natural Law in its stead. This is a world, as Matthew Arnold characterised it in 'Dover Beach' (1851), where "the Sea of Faith" is known by its "melancholy, long withdrawing roar," and where the world we are left with "Hath really neither joy, nor love, nor light,/ Nor certitude, nor peace, nor help for pain."

Of course others rushed in to fill the vacuum left by the withdrawal of orthodox Christianity. The second half of the 19th century is more than usually full of crackpot religions and sects, of Mediums who promised to put the living in touch with the dead, and of all sorts of frauds, hucksters and the plain deluded. One west-country man believed himself to be God. He insisted that letters sent to him be addressed to "The Lord God, Somerset." Otherwise sane people fell into the clutches of bogus individuals and communities. Yeats accepted Madame Blavatsky's preposterous claims (including the ability to produce ectoplasm) and was for most of his life a member of the Theosophical Society of the Golden Dawn; Laurence Oliphant handed over his money and his wife to the Thomas Lake Harris Brotherhood and lived to regret it; Sir Arthur Conan Doyle was for a while President of the Society of Psychical Research (he believed the two Yorkshire girls who not only claimed to have seen fairies at the bottom of their garden but had the photographs to prove it); and, before any of them, Elizabeth Barrett Browning became convinced that the American medium, Daniel Dunglas Home (1833-1886), was the genuine article. Her husband, who had witnessed Home conducting a séance in London in 1855, had no doubt that the man was a fraud.

'Mr Sludge, "The Medium"' is set in the United States, which Browning never visited. There is no need to regard the poem as anti-American, although British travellers to the States usually went avowing their enthusiasm for the promise of a world made new, and returned with markedly different feelings. Even Dickens, who set out early in 1842 for America ardent in his determination to champion the Republic, became increasingly disenchanted. His disillusionment is set out both in *American Notes* (1842) and *Martin Chuzzlewit* (1844). the novel in which he excoriates those who gulled the innocent into parting with their money and goods. Frauds, conmen, rainmakers:

they contaminate the America of his novel, though it has to be said that Dickens is no more severe than Mark Twain was to be on the king and the duke in *Huckleberry Finn* (1884).

Mr Sludge makes no bones about admitting that he's a cheat. But he has an explanation. As always, the monologue opens in media res. He's been caught out by the person he addresses:

> Now, don't, sir! Don't expose me! Just this once!
> This was the first and only time, I'll swear, –
> Look at me, – see, I kneel, – the only time,
> I swear, I ever cheated, – yes, by the soul
> Of Her who hears – (your sainted mother, sir!)
> All, except this last accident, was truth –
> This little kind of slip! – and even this,
> (It was your own wine, sir, the good champagne,
> I took it for Catawba, you're so kind)
> Which put the folly in my head!

And so, by a mixture of panic, hypocritical appeal – "your sainted mother", self-exculpation ("it was your own wine, sir") and greasy compliment ("you're so kind") Mr Sludge comes before us. By the end of the poem however, he's a good deal more confident, suggesting on the one hand that though he cheated, "there was something in it, tricks and all!", and on the other that if he cheated, well, he was only doing the same as others:

> What need I care? I cheat in self-defence,
> And there's my answer to a world of cheats!
> Cheat? To be sure, sir! What's the world worth else?
> Who takes it as he finds, and thanks his stars?
>
> (lls 1346-9)

If necessity is the tyrant's plea, the conman's is that of universal amorality. And so buoyed up is Sludge by this conclusion that with magnificent, Uriah Heep-like magnanimity he even forgives the man who has caught him cheating. "There, sir! I bear no malice: 'tisn't in me."

But just in case we might miss the point, Browning at last leaves him on his own to rave at the injustice of it all, and, moreover, to plan his revenge. He'll make up a story to turn to turn the tables on his accuser:

> I too can tell my story: brute, – do you hear? –
> You throttled your sainted mother, that old hag,
> In just such a fit of passion: no, it was ...
> To get this house of hers, and many a note
> Like these ... I'll pocket them, however ... five,
> Ten, fifteen ... ay, you gave her throat the twist,
> Or else you poisoned her!
>
> (11s 1505-11)

From this, improvising like Iago, he goes on to imagine telling the story to others, its details more lurid by the moment:

> I said he poisoned her,
> And hoped he'd have grace given him to repent,
> Whereon he picked this quarrel, bullied me
> And called me cheat: I thrashed him, – who could help?
> He howled for mercy, prayed me on his knees
> To cut and run and save him from disgrace:
> I do so, and once off, he slanders me.
>
> (11s 1515-21)

And so the crook transmutes himself in his own hectic imagination into a man of probity, a moral hero. This is how bare-faced liars work to ensure Captive good will attend Captain ill.

'Mr Sludge, "The Medium"' runs to over 1500 lines. If we leave aside the early Shelleyan epics, *Pauline*, *Paracelsus* and *Sordello*, it is the longest poem Browning had so far written and is different from them in being a dramatic monologue. It is one of Browning's finest, fit to stand comparison with 'The Bishop Orders His Tomb'. And as with that poem, the protagonist is so wonderfully brought before us, so alive in the twistings and turnings of his mind, in the multiple ways he betrays himself, that when we contemplate what art went into his making we have surely to say that Browning's only peers in this regard are Shakespeare and Dickens. (Dickens had a great regard for Browning, and was especially impressed by what he considered to be the dramatic genius of Browning's play, *A Blot In The 'Scutcheon*.) It was an art he would take to still greater heights when he came to write *The Ring and the Book*.

Two further poems bring *Dramatis Personae* to a close, 'Apparent Failure' and then, last of all, 'Epilogue'. Of this latter poem Pettigrew and Collins say that its "importance as a statement of Browning's religious position is universally recognised." This is so. Perhaps the best account of the poem is to be found in Philip Drew's study of Browning's Poetry. Drew notes that the three speakers in the poem represent three views of Christianity. The first, called David, tries to locate God in His Church, though his view is rejected by the others. Indeed, the second, profoundly pessimistic speaker, concludes that Christ's death is final. There will be no Second Coming. Significantly, this speaker is called Renan. Browning's first readers would have known that Ernest Renan (1823-1892) was the author of the *Vie de Jesus*, which made an enormous stir across Europe when it was published in 1863, because in it Renan identified Christ as an historical figure but, using scholarly arguments, denied him divine status.

The third, unnamed, speaker in the 'Epilogue' contrasts the search for God without the Self to the search for God within. This, Drew maintains, had by 1864 become Browning's own position. And he adds that the 'Epilogue' "records how far Browning had moved … from anything that might be called orthodox Christianity." I quote this, not because I am especially interested in the 'Epilogue', but for the sake of the poem that comes before it.

'Apparent Failure' carries as epigraph a report from a Paris newspaper, "We shall soon lose a celebrated building". The building in question, a morgue where suicides were taken, was scheduled for immediate demolition. 'Apparent Failure' starts with the dramatic declaration "No, for I'll save it!". The poem that follows was one of Tennyson's favourites, but has never been much discussed by Browning's critics. Perhaps it embarrasses them? Philip Drew quotes DeVane's remark that in *Dramatis Personae* Browning "almost alone wrote of contemporary ideas and contemporary life, often in a colloquial language and contemporary phrase", and says that the point can be illustrated "on a simple level by observing that one poem, 'Apparent Failure', was *based on* a newspaper item about the threatened demolition of the Paris morgue". He adds: "but the more interesting signs of modernity are less obvious than this." Well, yes, they are, but it is surely unfair to describe the poem as *based on* a newspaper item? The quotation is the poem's starting-point, that is all. Drew gives the impression that Browning is versifying a piece of journalism, and although this might or might not be an "obvious" way of getting "contemporary ideas and contemporary life" into poetry, it is not what Browning does. I suspect that Drew's feeling about the poem – that it is "obvious" – springs from a hasty reading and a belief that 'Apparent Failure' shows Browning at his bluffest, breeziest and most gratingly insensitive.

W.O. Raymond is one of the very few critics to have written about the poem with anything like enthusiasm. And if he is right then there is certainly much cause for concern. Speaking of Browning's religious position, Raymond claims that the poet "does not qualify the optimism of his absolute idealism":

> For Browning, 'all things ill' are not, as Milton regarded them, merely 'slavish officers of vengeance' in the service of 'the Supreme Good'; they are rather, through being transmuted, the slavish officers of God's love. Ultimately, since God is omnipotent as well as all-loving, every sinner, through remorse, repentance, atonement, and divine mercy, must be redeemed. Such a belief involves the rejection of the doctrine of eternal punishment. Confronted with an appalling aftermath of evil in the bodies of three suicides lying in the Paris morgue, Browning writes in "Apparent Failure" …

And Raymond then quotes the poem's final stanza in the belief that it fully endorses his account of Browning's beliefs. In a sense I suppose that it does. But where Raymond sees a praiseworthy optimism I find something closer to that "smug Christian optimism worthy of a dissenting grocer" to which Hardy memorably referred. And of course we can find its equivalent elsewhere in the poem:

> I plucked up heart and entered, – stalked,
> Keeping a tolerable face
> Compared with some whose cheeks were chalked:
> Let them! No Briton's to be baulked!

A strong whiff of Podsnappery hangs over those words, the smack of those rhymes, those thumping exclamations. They remind me of Lady St Helier's claim that Browning "spoke louder, and with greater persistency than anyone I have ever come across in my life." And we might look at other lines, and wonder:

> The reverence struck me; o'er each head
> Religiously was hung its hat,
>   Each coat dripped by the owner's bed
> Sacred from touch …

Religiously, sacred: the words are emphasised by their positioning. Could irony be more tasteless?

At a glance 'Apparent Failure' may well seem to be the poem which above all others advertises the insensitivity of Browning's beefy optimism, his emotional and intellectual vulgarity, his formal tactlessness, and in which these faults are at their most glaring because of the poem's subject. And this, I assume, is why Browning's more tactful critics tend to glide past the poem.

Yet the poem's virtue rests precisely in its monumental tastelessness – or rather in the way such tastelessness comes to be recognised as it collides with something else that is markedly present in 'Apparent Failure', an extraordinarily sensitive range of feelings that are called out by what Browning has to say about the three suicides. Collision is the essence. Again and again sensitivity and insensitivity come together:

> And this – why, he was red in vain,
>   Or black, – poor fellow that is blue!

The flexibility of these rhythms is that of a considerate attentiveness. Speak the lines and the quality of Browning's regard is at once obvious. And yet it seems fatally demeaned by the ghastly joke about colours. How to explain it? And more important, how to justify it?

Certainly not by endorsing Raymond's view of the poem. Here, it may help to insert a piece of autobiography. I first came across 'Apparent Failure' when I was 19. I had been reading an essay on George Orwell on the Spanish Civil War, in the course of which Orwell said that the "Spanish Republic failed, having gained what no republic missed". The remark seemed oddly obscure for so lucid a writer. I showed it to one of my lecturers. "Browning", he said, "it comes from a poem of Browning's". He couldn't remember which poem but after some searching I found it and read 'Apparent Failure' for the first time. It bowled me over. It also more or less formed my introduction to Browning's poetry which until then and apart from some obvious anthology pieces I had hardly so much as glanced at. And this is important. For I did not know that Browning's 'official' account of the universe was held in contempt by contemporary critics and poets. I knew nothing of his "smug dissenting" optimism. Nor did I find it in 'Apparent Failure'. What I did find was a poem that showed its speaker to be in an absurd but dramatic and moving muddle, a man who wanted to find some value or significance in the experience he had undergone, but who was forced to admit that the only 'meaning' he could make out of his encounter with death felt at best inadequate, at worst absurd. It was such an *honest* poem. There was no doubting the genuineness of the shock of that encounter, and indeed the shock felt all the more genuine just because it couldn't be tamed. Instead, the poet tried to retreat from the experience into cleverness, tried to cope by pushing a screen of tricksy words between himself and the fact of death. And the jarring quality of that smart-alec language made even plainer his sense of shock. Since then I have re-read the poem at regular intervals, and I am convinced that my first response to it was the correct one. I do not doubt that optimism is present in 'Apparent Failure', but it seems to me perfectly obvious that it is on trial there, and that our verdict on it is unfavourable because Browning allows us to see how vulnerable it is in the face of his experience. Indeed, the poem as a whole is about vulnerability. That is part of its honesty.

We begin with a parodic image of the Englishman abroad, all bluster and hot certainties. The poem hauls us in, with its brisk, no-nonsense air. (Hardy learned much from Browning in the matter of getting poems under way). The conversational, informal manner is important. It allows us to infer a good deal about this man for whom all life seems a meal spread out for the tasting. A baptism in Paris, and then on to fresh experiences: life is to be eagerly savoured. I "Saw, made my bow, and went my way". "So sauntered till – what met my eyes?" Our appetite is whetted by the question. We are hooked. And into stanza II we go, accompanying this man eager for experience – this time of looking at the bodies of suicides:

> Only the Doric little Morgue!
> The dead-house where you show your drowned:

> Petrarch's Vaucluse makes proud the Sorgue,
>> Your Morgue has made the Seine renowned.
> One pays one's debt in such a case;
>> I plucked up heart and entered, – stalked,
> Keeping a tolerable face
>> Compared with some whose cheeks were chalked:
> Let them! No Briton's to be balked!

"I plucked up heart and entered". Oh, no you didn't, I want to protest. No one who puts it like that has to pluck up heart – the phrase is merely a conventional bow in the direction of a conventional attitude to death. And how conventional an Englishman this man is, with his contempt for "some whose cheeks were chalked".

But in stanza III the voice begins to lose something of its strident bounce. And there is, surely, a shade of uneasy delay about coming face-to-face with the dead men? A succession of phrases thrust themselves between us and the suicides: "the sight's self, the sermon's text". Yes, yes, but what *is* the text? And then we get it, in language that is altogether stripped and bare. "The three men who did most abhor/ Their life in Paris yesterday,/ So killed themselves". The terse, uncompromising starkness of that last half-line is in complete contrast to the bluff playing with words that had preceded it. No room for Podsnappery now:

> Each on his copper couch, they lay
>> Fronting me, waiting to be owned.

"Copper couch". It is shade brutal, the clang of consonant almost comically macabre. Difficult to be entirely honest in the face of death. Or rather, honesty involves some recognition of the ridiculous indignity of the dead men. Yet after all they are waiting to be owned. And not just by relatives. The word releases a great deal of meaning: Browning must own to his shared identity with these men, for they also are or were human; and death is the final truth to which he must own up, for all his bully-boy swagger. The pathos of the suicides derives from their isolation, of not being owned by or belonging to anyone. And perhaps the men chose death because they felt themselves utterly alone and unloved, and so paradoxically – but understandably – died in order to bring themselves to the attention of others. '*Now* will you own that I existed!' "I thought, and think, their sin's atoned." This does not seem to me a line of pious optimism. The men atoned for their sin by dying and becoming hopelessly vulnerable to the stares of the living, becoming among other things ridiculous in death.

This is not to deny that the line has obvious Christian connotations. But it is to say that as we move into stanza IV we notice how blasphemous the connotations feel. Are these men really God-made, and if so what are we to think of God? The following words have my own emphasis:

> The *reverence* struck me; o'er each head
> *Religiously* was hung its hat,
>   Each coat dripped by the owner's bed
> *Sacred* from touch …

What kind of reverence is this? Surely the dispassionate care of the morgue's attendants in seeing to it that the right items are put by each dead man is a fearful mockery of human civility, a pointless exercise in preserving individuality? But in registering the insensitivity of Browning's language we understand that in fact he is trying to keep a 'balanced' view of death by making a joke and also reporting what is itself a joke of the blackest kind, the 'religious' treatment of the dead men's clothes. "Each had his proper place of rest." Proper? The word is a vicious pun on propriety. Yet it also blankly asserts that perhaps it *is* proper, perhaps death *is* best for them. Which idea, though certainly not in line with Christian optimism, is taken further in the next two stanzas.

Both stanzas V and VI ponder the cause of suicide, and stanza V exhibits a real tenderness of regard for the dead men. The tone of this stanza, muted, almost affectionate, is in sharp contrast to the loud self-regard of the poem's opening. Not that Browning can actually know what led them to take their own lives; but he dignifies their deaths – if anything can – by his speculations. "You wanted to be Buonaparte/ And have the Tuileries for toy." To fail in such a dream is heroic, might be worth breaking your heart over; and though the tone properly catches up the wryness of such speculation, there is no withdrawal of sympathy. So, too, with the old leveller. "Be quiet, and unclench your fist!" Almost comic, it yet pays its tribute to the man's restless and untameable spirit. Language is doing what it can to attend to the *fact* of death and at the same time discover what can be said for life.

But the tone is very different in stanza VI, which must be one of the finest and most troubling pieces of verse that Browning ever wrote:

> And this – why, he was red in vain,
>> Or black, – poor fellow that is blue!
> What fancy was it turned your brain?
>> Oh, women were the prize for you!
> Money gets women, cards and dice
>> Get money, and ill-luck gets just
> The copper couch and one clear nice
>> Cool squirt of water o'er your bust,
> The right thing to extinguish lust!

It is not at all easy to pin down the tone of this stanza. Hard, brutal almost: the words are appropriate, but insufficient. Panache? Yes, the stanza has panache in the way it moves with coolly dramatic suavity through the last five lines. It is a very unsettling stanza. This is partly because Browning's very suavity, his pleasure in getting the stanza down – and he must have taken pleasure in the manner he can use the word "Get" for example – seems pretty nasty. But then nastiness is the point. The clear, logical way the stanza unfolds, records the fact that suicide can itself be the logical outcome of a certain way of life. Of course life *can* be rich, mysterious, many-sided. It can also lead straight to the copper couch. And in that extraordinary last line Browning feels almost to be sharing a sardonic joke with the dead man. Now that he has so clearly unwound the path to his death, the poet sees the man's suicide not as tragedy – made out of a broken heart of restless despair – but merely as the product of ill-luck. Those words suggest both a run of ill-fortune at the gambling-tables and perhaps with women, and even a miscalculation over the death itself. Which I readily agree is not the sort of thing we expect Browning to be saying, but nevertheless is what he says here. It is shocking – and we see now how the joke about colours helps the overall effect – because Browning is prepared to admit that life can be seen as an absurd joke.

The final stanza is comparatively straightforward:

It's wiser being good than bad;
 It's safer being meek than fierce:
It's fitter being sane than mad.
 My own hope is, a sun will pierce
The thickest cloud earth ever stretched;
 That, after Last, returns the First,
Though a wide compass round be fetched;
 That what began best, can't end worst,
Nor what God blessed once, prove accurst.

Or is it? For this can, I think, be read in different ways. We may see the stanza as aggressively and insensitively optimistic, or as resigned, or as Smilesian. Or as blank, uncomprehending, its platitudes masking a bleakly pessimistic account of life. I think we have to see it as *all* these things. "My own hope is". Yes, but the more you look at that phrase and what follows it, and then think back into the poem, the less chance does there seem for such a hope to be other than whistling in the dark. And this is the nub of the matter. For in its very real vulnerability, its laying itself open to severe questioning and its readiness to be scorned, the phrase indicates where the strength of 'Apparent Failure' lies. Language cannot finally tame the fact of death.

6   The Later Years

Following the comparative success of *Dramatis Personae*, Browning's reputation began to rise, and he was increasingly read and written about. A cynic might say that his fame increased as his poetry declined. But this would be wrong. Although there is nothing in the later collections to match the overall achievement of *Men and Women*, Browning was still capable of good work. There is, though, something strained about the later poetry, which is inadvertently hinted at in what seems to me the increasingly desperate jocosity of the titles he gave to each successive collection. Simply to set these down is to recognise as much. In 1871 he published both *Balaustin's Adventure* and *Prince Hohenstiel-Schwangau*, then, in quick succession *Fifine at the Fair* (1872) and *Red Cotton Night-Cap Country, or Turf and Towers* (1873), an enormous and, if truth be told, bloated novel in verse, based on a story Browning had heard while on holiday in France in 1872, about a man who killed himself in remorse for "having behaved unfilially to his mother." Once he had examined the evidence surrounding the circumstances of his death, Browning became convinced that the man had no intention of committing suicide, although "religious considerations" had played their part in his fall from a tower on his estate in Normandy. Pettigrew and Collins remark that the poem had few admirers and is "but seldom read; some readers also find the tone, with its grotesque blend of savage humour, whimsical humour and intense seriousness, difficult to adjust to." Agreed.

Red Cotton Night-Cap Country is a thing to wonder over, not merely because it is *so* grotesque, but because it demonstrates such energy. It and *Fifine at the Fair* both come after *The Ring and the Book*, a huge and hugely magnificent novel in verse that Browning began writing in 1864, finished in the Spring of 1868, and published in four parts between that autumn and the following Spring. In Richard Altick's excellent Penguin edition, *The Ring and the Book* runs to over 600 pages, which would be enough to count as the life's work of most other poets. But although it is by far and away the best production of Browning's later years, and a work about which I shall have something more to say, *The Ring and the Book* is merely one of a host of undertakings that continued almost without break until the poet's death.

After Red Cotton Night-Cap Country come *Aristophanes 'Apology*, and *The Inn Album* (both 1875), *Pacchiarotto and How He Worked in Distemper* (1876) and, among much else, a version of *The Agamemnon of Aeschylus* (1877), two collections of *Dramatic Idylls* (1879 and 1880), *Jocoseria* (1883), *Ferishtah's Fancies* (1884), *Parleyings with Certain People of Importance in Their Day* (1887) and finally – it was published in the day of his death, 12 December 1889 *Asolando*. With the exception of a fine essay by Peter Porter on *The Parleyings*, I don't know of any interesting criticism on these late collections, nor can I imagine that, outside specialist circles, any criticism, of whatever worth, is likely to be forthcoming. Porter notes that the word 'parleying' offers a clue to Browning's style. It is, he says, "perfectly comprehensible, meaning talking to a person or persons, but it is also slightly archaic, not exactly formal but smacking of discursiveness, of a tendency to holding forth, perhaps even of not listening very carefully to any reply."

Among those with whom Browning parleys in 1887 are Daniel Bartoli, an Italian Jesuit historian (1609-85), and the politician George Bubb Doddington (1691-1762), a tricky customer Pope (who satirised him as 'Bufo') detested and whom Browning uses as a stalking horse to attack Disraeli. Browning loathed Disraeli for his deviousness. But the most interesting parleying is, I think, with Christopher Smart, whose 'Song to David' Browning apparently knew by heart. It has been suggested that Browning uses Smart to point a contrast with his own younger contemporaries of the "fleshly school of poetry", the aesthetes, especially Swinburne, who promoted "art for art's sake." This may be so, although by the time Browning came to write his poem the row about Swinburne and Rossetti's 'decadence', which had flared up in 1871 and continued intermittently throughout the 1870s, had more or less died down. It would be reignited in the 1890s, of course, but Browning wasn't to know that. What he did know was that certain modern poets, including such now forgotten figures as Edwin Arnold and Robert Montgomery, made vast claims for their poetry on the basis of a kind of cosmic awareness. And so he imagines them claiming that:

> 'We scale the skies, then drop
> To earth – to find, how all things there are loth
> To answer heavenly law: we understand
> The meteor's course, and, lo, the rose's growth –
> How other than should be by law's command!'

If Browning does have Swinburne partly in mind here, it is less Swinburne the aesthete than Swinburne the atheist. Understanding the meteor's course means understanding laws of gravity and planetary movement and thus acknowledging science as the true interpreter of the universe. In 1874, in what became known as the Belfast Address, John Tyndall, then President of the British Association of Scientists, told his fellows:

> The impregnable position of science may be described in a few words. We claim, and we shall wrest from theology, the entire domain of cosmological theory. All schemes and systems which thus infringe upon the domain of science must, in so far as they do this, submit to its control, and relinquish all thought of controlling it.

The confidence – arrogance? – of this claim made a profound affect not merely on Tyndall's audience but on all those who were to read his words. The poet whom Browning imagines speaking with such certainty in the lines quoted above is plainly on Tyndall's side. Smart, however, just as plainly isn't. Hence, his answering words, with which the poem comes to its end:

> Friends, beware lest fume
> Obfuscate sense: learn earth first ere presume
> To teach heaven legislation. Law must be
> Active in earth or nowhere: earth you see, –
> Or there or not at all, Will, Power, and Love
> Admit discovery, – as below, above
> Seek law's next confirmation! ...
> Live and learn
> Not first learn and then live, is our concern.

It is not difficult to imagine these words being quoted for approval by the Browning Society, which had been set up in 1881 with the explicit aim of establishing Browning as *A Philosophical and*

Religious Teacher, to quote the title of a study of the poet by Professor Henry Jones ("Professor of Philosophy at the University of Glasgow") published two years after Browning's death. In *Literature and Dogma* (1873) Matthew Arnold had prophesied that "more and more we shall turn to literature to interpret life for us"; the Browning Society wanted to recruit their poet for precisely that purpose. This may explain why, in the *Parleyings*, Browning himself seems to want to bring false prophets to heel, whether religious, political or scientific.

Parleyings with Certain People is the best of Browning's late work, although there is something to be said for one or two of the poems that make up *Asolando*, especially perhaps 'Muckle-Mouth Meg', a rumbustious retelling of a story that Walter Scott had made famous in *Tales of a Grandfather*, of an Englishman who will be saved from the gallows on condition that he agrees to marry Meg, she of the huge mouth. He refuses:

> 'Life's sweet: shall I say ye wed Muckle-Mouth Meg?'
> 'Not I' quoth the stout heart: 'too eerie
> The mouth that can swallow a bubblejock's egg:
> Shall I let it maunch mine? Never, Dearie!'

"Bubblejock" is Scottish for a turkey-cock. The poem seems to have been written in June, 1889, that is, in Browning's 78th year. There is something joyously reassuring in knowing that he could come by so ebullient a poem as 'Muckle-Mouth Meg' in his extreme old age. Reading it, I think of Yeats' vision of the ancient Chinamen in 'Lapis Lazuli', and of how "Their eyes mid many wrinkles, their eyes,/ Their ancient, glittering eyes, are gay."

As for *The Ring and the Book*, this great work needs a study to itself. Henry James was among the first to recognise its stature and he wrote about it at length. James thought of the work as essentially a novel, and he perhaps unsurprisingly makes it sound like one of his own. (Although he significantly suggests ways in which the work could have been re-written and so improved.) But whatever his demurs, James was much influenced by the subtlety of Browning's psychological insights into those of his characters he studies (and exposes) in dramatic monologue. Chesterton adds to James' account by saying of the *Ring and the Book* that "it is the epic of free speech." No matter how many later critics have written about the book, all have followed the template James and Chesterton laid down. The essential thing about *The Ring and the Book* is that it is a great device for using a number of dramatic monologues in order to bring before us different points of view about a single event. As everyone notices, the work is a detective story. What they don't notice is that it bears some comparison to Wilkie Collins' *The Woman in White* (1861) which uses different narrative devices to make the truth problematic. And of course Collins' super-subtle villain is the Italian Count Fosco.

The story of *The Ring and the Book* is in a sense reminiscent of 'My Last Duchess'. We are back in Renaissance Italy, and made to peer in as spectators at the gradual unearthing of what Browning called the "curious depth below depth of depravity" he had found in an old yellow book picked up on a stall in Florence. That told of the murder of a young wife, Pompilia, by her husband, Guido, and of his attempt to disguise the truth of what he had done. The truth eventually comes out, and that it does so depends on the intuitions of the Pope, before whom Guido has to plead his case, as much as on any hard information the Pope has to hand. Even then, Guido expects to be let off. But no, he is executed, although significantly not in the usual place reserved for executions, but in the Square frequented by the nobility. "So shall the quality see, fear and learn." I am fascinated by the fact that in both Collins' novel and Browning's poem, the evil-doers are from the aristocracy, or gentry, 'the quality' or those who would pretend to such status. I think we would be right to infer from this that both writers are in their own ways sensitive to a newly emerging discontent with the aristocracy, and are sympathetically alert to the stirrings of a challenge to presumptions of aristocratic privilege. And in this context it is certainly proper to note comparisons between *The Ring and the Book* and Shelley's play, *The Cenci* (1819), which Browning greatly admired, although Shelley made much of Papal wickedness, whereas Browning's Pope is presented on the whole sympathetically. Where they are alike is, of course, in their exposure of nobility as having no sense of *oblige*.

To say this is to be reminded that Browning was from first to last a democratic republican. By the time he died he had lost faith – or perhaps patience – with Shelley, having become disenchanted with the great Sun-treader's way of life as that had been set out in Edward Dowden's biography of 1881. Matthew Arnold was not merely disenchanted, he was aghast at Dowden's revelations. "What a set, what a world", he famously expostulated. Browning didn't go that far but he was undoubtedly shocked by Shelley's treatment of various women, especially his first wife, Harriet. It might be possible to see in this either an undue uxoriousness or an element of 'Victorian' prudishness. But it is, I suggest, far better to recognise Browning's response to Shelley's casual and self-serving behaviour as at one with those many sympathetic studies of women that throng the pages of his (Browning's) work. And if Guido's place of execution is chosen to make the "quality see, fear, and learn", among the things they have to learn is not merely the legitimacy of democratic aspirations but the rights of women.

Further Reading

The best edition of Browning's poems is undoubtedly that by John Pettigrew and Thomas J. Collins ("Supplemented and Completed by", according to the title page), Penguin, 2 volume, 1981. The edition is well annotated and invaluably follows Browning's ordering of his poems. The best edition of the *Ring and the Book*, also in Penguin, is by Richard Altick, 1971.

There are several modern biographies of Browning, including one by Betty Miller, whose attempt to prove Browning found himself in a kind of Oedipal relationship with his wife is sometimes entertaining and often procrustean, and another by Park Honan, which is dogged. By far the best is that by John Woolford and Daniel Karlin, who write well about the poems as well as providing a good account of Browning's life and times (1996).

As to criticism: G.K. Chesterton's study, first published in 1903, seems to me an unimprovably good piece of work, a masterpiece in its own right. W.C. De Vane's *A Browning Handbook* (second edn. 1955) is an indispensable reference work for dates, sources and information about the contemporary reception of Browning's poems. Philip Drew's *The Poetry of Robert Browning, A Critical Introduction* (1971) is thorough if uninspiring, and there are useful essays to be found in *Robert Browning* (Writers and their Background), edited by Isobel Armstrong, 1974. Roma A. King's *The Bow and the Lyre: The Art of Robert Browning* (1964) is not without merit. I also recommend the Casebook *Men and Women and Other Poems* ed. J.R. Watson (1974). However, the best writing on Browning, Chesterton apart, is to be found in books devoted to more general issues of 19th century poetry. Chief among these are: Robert Langbaum's *The Poetry of Experience: The Dramatic Monologue in Modern Literary Tradition*, first published in 1957 but still one of the best of all accounts of a key aspect of Browning's poetry (Langbaum's chapter on *The Ring and the Book* is outstanding); E.D.H. Johnson's *The Alien Vision of Victorian Poetry* (1962), is interesting on the tensions between what might be called the sense of social responsibility and personal preference in the poets about whom he writes, Browning included; J. Hillis Miller's, *The Disappearance of God: Five 19th Century Writers* (1963) which flits about Browning's poetry by way of trying to judge his quarrel with religion; J.W. Harper's 'Eternity is our Due; Time in the Poetry of Robert Browning', an interesting essay to be found in the 1972 Stratford-Upon-Avon-Studies, devoted to *Victorian Poetry*, and edited by Malcolm Bradbury and David Palmer; *The Heart's_Events: The Victorian Poetry of Relationships*, by Patricia M. Ball (1976) – Ball is especially good on 'James Lee's Wife'; John Lucas' *England and Englishness: Poetry and Nationhood, 1688-1900*, which discusses Browning's Republicanism as part of his radicalism (and hence feminism), and Isobel Armstrong, whose recent full-length study of *Victorian Poetry* (1996) makes excellent use of the latest critical thinking about Browning as well as adding much of importance on her own account. Finally, Peter Porter's *Saving From the Wreck: Essays on Poetry*, (2001) has a first-rate essay on 'Browning's Important Parleying' as well as any number of astute remarks about Browning scattered throughout his book.

GREENWICH EXCHANGE BOOKS

Greenwich Exchange Student Guides are critical studies of major or contemporary serious writers in English and selected European languages. The series is for the student, the teacher and 'common readers' and is an ideal resource for libraries. The *Times Educational Supplement* (*TES*) praised these books, saying, "The style of these guides has a pressure of meaning behind it. Students should learn from that ... If art is about selection, perception and taste, then this is it."

(ISBN prefix 1-871551-   applies)
The series includes:
W.H. Auden by Stephen Wade (-36-6)
Honoré de Balzac by Wendy Mercer (48-X)
William Blake by Peter Davies (-27-7)
The Brontës by Peter Davies (-24-2)
Robert Browning by John Lucas (59-5)
Samuel Taylor Coleridge by Andrew Keanie (-64-1)
Joseph Conrad by Martin Seymour-Smith (-18-8)
William Cowper by Michael Thorn (-25-0)
Charles Dickens by Robert Giddings (-26-9)
John Donne by Sean Haldane (-23-4)
Thomas Hardy by Sean Haldane (-35-1)
Seamus Heaney by Warren Hope (-37-4)
Philip Larkin by Warren Hope (-35-8)
Laughter in the Dark – The Plays of Joe Orton by Arthur Burke (56-0)
Philip Roth by Paul McDonald (72-2)
Shakespeare's Non-Dramatic Poetry by Martin Seymour-Smith (22-6)
Shakespeare's Sonnets by Martin Seymour Smith (38-2)
Tobias Smollett by Robert Giddings (-21-8)
Alfred Lord Tennyson by Michael Thorn (-20-X)
William Wordsworth by Andrew Keanie (57-9)

OTHER GREENWICH EXCHANGE BOOKS
Paperback unless otherwise stated.

Shakespeare's Sonnets
Martin Seymour-Smith
Martin Seymour-Smith's outstanding achievement lies in the field of literary biography and criticism. In 1963 he produced his comprehensive edition, in the old spelling, of *Shakespeare's Sonnets* (here revised and corrected by himself and Peter Davies in 1998). With its landmark introduction and

its brilliant critical commentary on each sonnet, it was praised by William Empson and John Dover Wilson. Stephen Spender said of him "I greatly admire Martin Seymour-Smith for the independence of his views and the great interest of his mind"; and both Robert Graves and Anthony Burgess described him as the leading critic of his time. His exegesis of the *Sonnets* remains unsurpassed.

2001 • 194 pages • ISBN 1-871551-38-2

English Language Skills
Vera Hughes
If you want to be sure, as a student, or in your business or personal life,) that your written English is correct, this book is for you. Vera Hughes' aim is to help you remember the basic rules of spelling, grammar and punctuation. 'Noun', 'verb', 'subject', 'object' and 'adjective' are the only technical terms used. The book teaches the clear, accurate English required by the business and office world. It coaches acceptable current usage and makes the rules easier to remember.
Vera Hughes was a civil servant and is a trainer and author of training manuals.

2002 • 142 pages • ISBN 1-871551-60-9

LITERARY CRITICISM

The Author, the Book and the Reader
Robert Giddings
This collection of essays analyses the effects of changing technology and the attendant commercial pressures on literary styles and subject matter. Authors covered include Charles Dickens, Tobias George Smollett, Mark Twain, Dr Johnson and John le Carré.

1991 • 220 pages • illustrated • ISBN 1-871551-01-3

Liar! Liar!: Jack Kerouac – Novelist
R.J. Ellis
The fullest study of Jack Kerouac's fiction to date. It is the first book to devote an individual chapter to every one of his novels. *On the Road*, *Visions of Cody* and *The Subterraneans* are reread in-depth, in a new and exciting way. *Visions of Gerard* and *Doctor Sax* are also strikingly reinterpreted, as are other daringly innovative writings, like 'The Railroad Earth' and his "try at a spontaneous *Finnegan's Wake*" – *Old Angel Midnight*. Neglected writings, such as *Tristessa* and *Big Sur*, are also analysed, alongside better-known novels such as *Dharma Bums* and *Desolation Angels*.

R.J. Ellis is Senior Lecturer in English at Nottingham Trent University.
1999 • 295 pages • ISBN 1-871551-53-6

BIOGRAPHY

The Good That We Do
John Lucas
John Lucas' book blends fiction, biography and social history in order to tell the story of his grandfather, Horace Kelly. Headteacher of a succession of elementary schools in impoverished areas of London, 'Hod' Kelly was also a keen cricketer, a devotee of the music hall, and included among his friends the great Trade Union leader, Ernest Bevin. In telling the story of his life, Lucas has provided a fascinating range of insights into the lives of ordinary Londoners from the First World War until the outbreak of the Second World War. Threaded throughout is an account of such people's hunger for education, and of the different ways government, church and educational officialdom ministered to that hunger. *The Good That We Do* is both a study of one man and of a period when England changed, drastically and forever.
John Lucas is Professor of English at Nottingham Trent University and is a poet and critic.
2001 • 214 pages • ISBN 1-871551-54-4

In Pursuit of Lewis Carroll
Raphael Shaberman
Sherlock Holmes and the author uncover new evidence in their investigations into the mysterious life and writing of Lewis Carroll. They examine published works by Carroll that have been overlooked by previous commentators. A newly discovered poem, almost certainly by Carroll, is published here.
Amongst many aspects of Carroll's highly complex personality, this book explores his relationship with his parents, numerous child friends, and the formidable Mrs Liddell, mother of the immortal Alice. Raphael Shaberman was a founder member of the Lewis Carroll Society and a teacher of autistic children.
1994 • 118 pages • illustrated • ISBN 1-871551-13-7

Musical Offering
Yolanthe Leigh
In a series of vivid sketches, anecdotes and reflections, Yolanthe Leigh tells the story of her growing up in the Poland of the 30s and the Second World War. These are poignant episodes of a child's first encounters with both the enchantments and the cruelties of the world; and from a later time, stark

memories of the brutality of the Nazi invasion, and the hardships of student life in Warsaw under the Occupation. But most of all this is a record of inward development; passages of remarkable intensity and simplicity describe the girl's response to religion, to music, and to her discovery of philosophy.

Yolanthe Leigh was formerly a Lecturer in Philosophy at Reading University.
2000 • 57 pages • ISBN: 1-871551-46-3

Norman Cameron
Warren Hope

Norman Cameron's poetry was admired by W.H. Auden, celebrated by Dylan Thomas and valued by Robert Graves. He was described by Martin Seymour-Smith as, "one of ... the most rewarding and pure poets of his generation ..." and is at last given a full length biography. This eminently sociable man, who had periods of darkness and despair, wrote little poetry by comparison with others of his time, but always of a consistently high quality – imaginative and profound.

2000 • 221 pages • illustrated • ISBN 1-871551-05-6

POETRY

Adam's Thoughts in Winter
Warren Hope

Warren Hope's poems have appeared from time to time in a number of literary periodicals, pamphlets and anthologies on both sides of the Atlantic. They appeal to lovers of poetry everywhere. His poems are brief, clear, frequently lyrical, characterised by wit, but often distinguished by tenderness. The poems gathered in this first book-length collection counter the brutalising ethos of contemporary life, speaking of and for the virtues of modesty, honesty and gentleness in an individual, memorable way.

2000 • 47 pages • ISBN 1-871551-40-4

Baudelaire: Les Fleurs du Mal
Translated by F.W. Leakey

Selected poems from *Les Fleurs du Mal* are translated with parallel French texts and are designed to be read with pleasure by readers who have no French as well as those who are practised in the French language.

F.W. Leakey was Professor of French in the University of London. As a scholar, critic and teacher he specialised in the work of Baudelaire for 50 years and published a number of books on the poet.

2001 • 153 pages • ISBN 1-871551-10-2

Lines from the Stone Age

Sean Haldane

Reviewing Sean Haldane's 1992 volume *Desire in Belfast*, Robert Nye wrote in *The Times* that "Haldane can be sure of his place among the English poets." This place is not yet a conspicuous one, mainly because his early volumes appeared in Canada and because he has earned his living by other means than literature. Despite this, his poems have always had their circle of readers. The 60 previously unpublished poems of *Lines from the Stone Age* – "lines of longing, terror, pride, lust and pain" – may widen this circle.

2000 • 53 pages • ISBN 1-871551-39-0

Wilderness

Martin Seymour-Smith

This is Martin Seymour-Smith's first publication of his poetry for more than 20 years. This collection of 36 poems is a fearless account of an inner life of love, frustration, guilt, laughter and the celebration of others. He is best known to the general public as the author of the controversial and bestselling *Hardy* (1994).

1994 • 52 pages • ISBN 1-871551-08-0